SYSTEMS OF
HIGHER EDUCATION
IN TWELVE
COUNTRIES

*The Praeger Special Studies
Series in Comparative Education*

*Published in Cooperation with the Comparative
Education Center, State University of New York, Buffalo*

General Editor: **Philip G. Altbach**

SYSTEMS OF HIGHER EDUCATION IN TWELVE COUNTRIES

A Comparative View

Nell P. Eurich

PRAEGER

PRAEGER SPECIAL STUDIES • PRAEGER SCIENTIFIC

Library of Congress Cataloging in Publication Data

Eurich, Nell.
    Systems of higher education in twelve countries.

    (The Praeger special studies series in comparative
education)
    Includes bibliographical references.
    1. Education, Higher—1965–   2. Higher educa-
tion and state. 3. Comparative education. I. Title.
II. Series: Praeger special studies series in comparative education.
LA183.E9   378   81–1245
ISBN 0–03–059391–3   AACR2

Published in 1981 by Praeger Publishers
CBS Educational and Professional Publishing
A Division of CBS, Inc.
521 Fifth Avenue, New York, New York 10175 U.S.A.

© 1981 by Praeger Publishers

123456789 145 987654321

Printed in the United States of America

The Praeger Special Studies Series in
Comparative Education
General Editor: **Philip G. Altbach**

Preface

In 1978 the International Council for Educational Development (ICED) published reports from 12 different countries, each one describing what was happening in higher education. All were part of a study to evaluate the effectiveness of systems emerging around the world: how they operate, what problems they are encountering, and the solutions being tried. This book summarizes the scene and compares the results. It is a composite view of major issues and efforts.

The 12 countries may seem an odd lot: Australia, Canada, France, the Federal Republic of Germany, Iran, Japan, Mexico, Poland, Thailand, Sweden, the United Kingdom, and the United States. They were not selected with carefully defined criteria in mind; in fact, they simply responded to an invitation and had leadership interested in participating. As it happens, the countries circle the globe, but all are in the northern hemisphere except Australia. Thus, there is no representation from the continents of Africa and South America. Such a study remains to be done in those important areas.

All countries adhered generally to guidelines provided for the study, except France where the report was based on a research project to gather selective opinion on current reforms in French higher education. The guidelines asked for 1) a description of the system, its size, and organization, 2) an evaluation of how it really operates, and 3) an evaluation of its flexibility, efficiency, and effectiveness in meeting goals. A copy of the guidelines is found in Appendix A.

It is immediately apparent that two-thirds of the study was evaluative and not quantitative. It called for the writers' opinions and any evidence they chose to give. In this aspect especially the study is unusual. Most comparative studies, particularly when so many countries are included, present a description, more or less factual, on each country. This one, in contrast, deals with more subjective and qualitative judgements. Furthermore, I have not hesitated to add my opinion on what is happening, what is missing, and the directions in which higher education is changing.

I have not drawn on other sources and interpretations of experts, but stayed with the material presented in the 12 countries' reports. There is more than enough substance in these reports alone, which also have the values of timeliness and structure from the study's framework. Thus, the study rests basically on a current view of the situation as seen by leaders of higher education in their own countries.

There is another feature that is somewhat different in this presentation. Instead of dealing separately with each country's higher education system and then concluding with a general comparison of their effectiveness, I have compared the different systems throughout the book in major aspects which constitute chapter titles: goals, government and funding, planning, coordination, academic autonomy, admissions, research, and innovation. While the traditional method for comparative studies might have lessened the likelihood of error, it would not have promoted consideration of trends and directions in which higher education is moving. This latter advantage seemed to me to outweigh the benefits of the safer approach. Without assumptions and projections, even if they prove wrong, we can do little to improve performance. Indeed, we cannot even create alternative possibilities.

Diversity among the countries challenges both generalizations and comparisons, but it does not defeat them. Many similarities exist in higher education systems, and frequently differences are only superficial. Above all, higher education shares problems which show little regard for national boundaries; they are epidemic across the lines drawn by historical circumstance.

Differences are more apt to appear clearly in the solutions that are being tried to cope with the problems. Responses are limited by a country's social and cultural background, its stage of economic development, and by political stance and leadership. Therefore, the analysis tends primarily toward comparison among the countries of their handling of the problems that beset all of them. Considering different solutions with their attendant mistakes and the new problems they create may be valuable to those in other countries who are contemplating similar developments. Perhaps it is too much to hope that we may learn from the errors of others, but at least there is the chance.

One country—Iran—requires special mention because its report was published a few months before the revolution early in 1979. It is included, like the others, since the report summarizes the status of Iranian higher education that the new regime inherited and on which it must build. Obviously, there can be few safe predictions on the future of Iran's higher education system.

There is the further question of defining *higher education* and *systems*. Both terms are elastic. Higher education is broadening to embrace many types of education beyond the traditional forms. Technical institutes, shorter forms of study, and various kinds of continuing education have lately been included in the concept of higher education. It has widened to mean all education at the tertiary level. This extension itself is a phenomenon indicating the more comprehensive view of higher education that governments are taking.

UNESCO follows a broad policy that classifies non-university institutions as third-level education for which completion of secondary school or its equivalent is necessary. Statistics include part-time students when possible, evening courses of the recognized level, correspondence courses in well-defined cases, and private as well as public institutions regardless of whether they confer university degrees. In the 1975 summary volume on *Classification of Educational Systems*, the Organization for Economic Cooperation and Development adopted UNESCO's definition for future studies, but five years later, UNESCO is still working on the complexities of an international standard classification.

For these reasons our study did not attempt a universally acceptable definition of higher education. Different countries have varying policies and changing definitions in practice. Significant evidence lies in the increasing use of the phrase "or its equivalent" whenever standards of achievement are mentioned for entrance in higher education.

The definition of higher education becomes doubly important for national planning, allocation of funds, and the structure of administration. Governments are widening the classification: they want the larger view in order to see their total financial commitment and the scope of higher education opportunities. Inside higher education, the view is commonly more narrow and is fragmented into categories like universities, two- or four-year colleges, technical and special institutes, and so on. The study concentrates on those categories presently incorporated in higher education systems, but specific reference is made to developments in the wider setting as they affect the established branches.

I might add that, because of the uncertainties over exactly what is included in the higher education category in various countries, I have not used comparative, quantitative tables. The data are simply not dependable on an international scale and are too apt to carry erroneous implications.

System has recently entered the vocabulary in higher education partly because of the fragmentation referred to among types of institutions. Most countries say they do not have a system of higher education; instead they have several systems, each for a type of institution, or they may consider higher education a system with subsystems or sectors for each type. Seldom is there one formal system operating coherently with organic parts that constitute an orderly whole. The search for such a system is in process. This is most apparent in the chapters on coordination and planning. I use the word *system* rather loosely as meaning the whole operation, recognizing it is not a formal structure but a scene with multiple parts or sectors that are interacting more and more frequently.

My deep appreciation goes to the most distinguished group of readers who participated in the ICED study: Burton R. Clark at the University of California at Los Angeles, Rune Premfors of Sweden, and Edward Sheffield of Canada for their helpful criticism of an early draft. I am especially indebted to Professor Lyman Glenny of Berkeley and Martin Meyerson, former President of the University of Pennsylvania, for painstaking analysis of a later draft. Their criticism was essential.

I also wish to thank James A. Perkins, Chairman of ICED, for the opportunity to work in this study under his wise and experienced leadership. It was a rare chance for me to learn a great deal. Now I only hope that the study may be valuable or at least provocative to others concerned with higher education around the world.

Contents

SYSTEMS OF
HIGHER EDUCATION
IN TWELVE
COUNTRIES

1
THE MILIEU

The 12 countries of the study—Australia, Canada, France, the Federal Republic of Germany, Iran, Japan, Mexico, Poland, Thailand, Sweden, the United Kingdom, and the United States—present a great mixture of completely unique characteristics and yet similarities that permit grouping them in types of one sort or another. Each has its own historical context in which the structure of higher education has taken shape and the program has evolved. Fashioned by a country's geographic location, its nature and size, historical events, religious, social and cultural attitudes, and political and economic developments, the higher education system, along with other social institutions, has emerged into what is now a more integrated world.

Some major problems and issues today confront all higher education systems regardless of their separate origins and distinctive characteristics. Their responses to the common problems retain the differences conditioned by their origin and development, while the problems reflect the growing international relationships of one society to another and the increasing speed at which issues encircle the civilized world. These common issues are discussed in subsequent chapters that show the range of solutions being tried by the individual countries.

At the same time, higher education, in any country, shares tasks common to all. Certain functions are basic, like teaching and research, and the fulfillment of individual abilities and society's needs. In this sense, goals for higher education become international, crossing the various national borders. Probably in no respect are the systems more alike than in statements of goals or, put affirmatively, goals are stated in much the same way by the different countries. Nevertheless, there are significant variations in emphasis and scope.

Before examining national goals, a preliminary glance at the broad spectrum of diversity represented by the countries is necessary. The view is cursory, but it serves as a reminder of the different contexts for the 12 higher education systems and as a caution against sweeping generalizations or grand summary statements.

HISTORY

The 12 countries have rather long histories, especially when Persia is remembered as the forerunner of Iran, and Siam as the precursor of Thailand, which took its present name only in 1949. With the historical view in mind, Iran can claim the earliest university, Jondishapur in Ahwaz, with faculties in philosophy, medicine, and pharmacy in the third century. Further, the Iranian report cites the existence of a "multicampus system" of seven campuses established in the eleventh century by Nezam el-Mulk in the Seljuk Empire. The institutions were financed largely by government, and students were provided room and board, with scholarships available for the needy. Of these institutions, the one at Isfahan survived until the early twentieth century.[1]

In the Western world, Oxford and the Sorbonne appeared in the twelfth and thirteenth centuries, respectively, and the universities at Heidelberg and Kraków in the fourteenth century. Uppsala University in Sweden followed in the next century. Moving to the Americas, the Spanish Crown established the Royal and Pontifical University of Mexico in 1551; and Canada and the United States, through private initiative, began higher institutions in the seventeenth century. Australia and Japan started universities in the nineteenth century that led modern developments, and Thailand in the twentieth.

Although the countries are spread over many centuries in the dates for their foundation of higher learning institutions, they are joined together in this century, particularly since World War II, in the phenomenal growth of such institutions and the numbers of students enrolled. Every one of them has experienced an enormous and unprecedented increase, making higher education an ever more important part of their economy and society.

GEOGRAPHY AND SIZE

The higher education systems of the study are in countries that differ dramatically in size—both in area and population—and resources. Canada is the largest in area with the United States and Australia next in that order. The United Kingdom and West Germany are the smallest and also have the greatest density of population per square mile with the exception, of course, of Japan. Yet, it is interesting to realize that Japan is considerably larger in terrritory than the other two, and even somewhat larger than Poland.

If density alone is compared, the range is staggering—from Japan's nearly 800 to Australia's not quite 5 people per square mile. And, probably little known, Iran has only about 5 more people per square mile than Sweden. Poland, moreover, a country smaller than Japan, has greater population density than Thailand or France.[2] Naturally the size of the population directly affects the size of the higher education system if the country is moving toward equality of opportunity as is true of every country in the ICED study. The birthrate and pattern of longevity with deathrates are further factors changing the marketplace for advanced learning by increasing or decreasing demand.

At present, most of these countries have lowered their birthrates, but Mexico, Iran, and Thailand continue to face the challenge of rapidly multiplying populations. Their systems of higher education are confronted with tremendous problems in numbers of people to be served now and in the future, as well as the need to offer a very wide variety of courses addressing the many social and technical areas for the development of their countries. On the other hand, those countries that have lowered birthrates now anticipate fewer students of the traditional age group in higher education and so face problems of an opposite sort—falling enrollments and subsequent cutbacks.

Concentration of population has also played a key part in the location of higher education institutions and the types of delivery systems needed to reach people. Following the natural environment, the Australian population is concentrated largely along the coastline while the central desert is sparsely populated. Most Canadians live within one hundred miles of the United States border, and the majority of Swedes live in the warmer, southern half of their kingdom. Universities and colleges tend to be grouped in the more populated regions. Consequently, the distribution of opportunities for advanced learning is often geographically distorted, and the higher education system is lopsided in the placement of its units.

The phenomenon of urbanization has compounded the natural flow of population and has centered huge masses of people in places like Bangkok, Teheran, and Mexico City. Earlier, other major capitals of the world experienced such growth with the problems attendant on becoming a megalopolis. In Thailand today, most of the government universities are located in Bangkok, and of the ten private colleges, only two are outside the metropolitan area. Rural areas are served primarily by government colleges.[3]

After World War II, one of the important reforms in Japanese higher education was to alleviate the concentration of universities in metropolitan areas and establish "at least one national university in each prefecture."[4]

Similarly, the French system has tried to reduce the drawing power of Paris and its environs which have attracted students disproportionately to that region.

Large and small countries alike are aware of the need to make higher education programs available to the people not now being adequately served. Even Poland and West Germany with relatively high population density patterns have the problem of developing regional opportunities. In the Swedish report, Rune Premfors comments directly on the influence of geographic and population factors:

> The geographical dispersion of institutions in Sweden corresponds closely to the distribution of the population. Although no systematic study has proven it, we are convinced that the 'population factor' has for long been decisive when institutions were founded.... Not until the late 1960s and work of U68 have considerations of regional development and social justice come to play an important role in public policy.[5]

Every country in the study recognizes the task of equalizing opportunity, not only economically and socially, but geographically for access. More than setting up additional institutions in less populated areas, "distance learning" and extension courses are gaining renewed attention, encouraged by the possibilities of technological media. The geographic dispersal of institutions is part of the basic design and organization of higher education systems just as population affects the size and nature of such systems.

Regional differences further condition the system's structure and functioning, especially when differences are marked and strongly held. In Canada, for example, the differences among the ten provinces are sufficiently sharp and distinct to prompt a regional presentation of the report with separate chapters from the Atlantic Provinces, Quebec, Ontario, and Western Canada. Each province is distinctive in its characteristics and in its system of higher education.

Such differences might be expected in the United States, but regional distinction is less apparent in organizational structures for higher education than the extraordinary diversity that exists among the 50 states. Variations are extremely wide in the size of systems and the numbers enrolled, in the combination of public and private institutions, in the position of state governments with regard to control, and in the structural forms of the systems.

Larger countries like Canada and the United States may inevitably have pronounced differences whether regional or by individual states, but small countries also exhibit similar differences. One needs only look at the United Kingdom's coalition of Scotland, Northern Ireland, Wales, and England. Over many years, the four regions have maintained unique characteristics.

Today Northern Ireland and Scotland have their own education departments that function somewhat differently from the others.

HOMOGENEITY AND DIVERSITY

Often related to regional differences within countries is the cultural composition of populations that naturally affects the higher education system. Demands upon higher education multiply with the diversity among the peoples of the society, and methods of operating within the system are affected as well. A relatively homogeneous population can, for example, act more easily on a consensus basis than a population made up of people from many diverse backgrounds. Such is the case in Sweden and Japan. Both operate from strong similarity and stability in their ethnic bases. Japan, closed to foreigners for more than a century, has built a society with a high degree of conformity in behavior and custom, and group identification is valued more than individualism. Decisions can be made through consultation and consensus.

On a scale ranging from homogeneity at one end to diversity at the other, most of the countries cluster toward the homogeneous end with the majority of their people relatively similar in ethnic background. West Germany, the United Kingdom, Poland, and Thailand rank fairly high on the uniform end of the scale. Australia is close with over 90 percent of the population of British origin. France, from an ethnic base of various European and Mediterranean groups, has created a remarkably homogenous and unified population.[6]

Mexico and Iran have greater mixtures and fall toward the middle of the scale. Canada reflects the notable bicultural combination of English and French which, at present, means that roughly three-quarters of their students in higher education are using the English language while the rest speak French.[7] Yet nearly one-fourth of Canada's population comes from other European countries and elsewhere.

The United States stands at the point of utmost diversity—wholly apart from the other countries in its circumstances of birth and growth. It is an extreme mixture of people from Britain, western and eastern Europe, Africa, Asia, Latin America, and Canada. Immigrants have literally come from north, south, east, and west, and the largest numbers now entering are Spanish-speaking from south of the border and the Caribbean Islands.

With this remarkable cultural mix, consensus could hardly be expected to operate; decisions perforce are determined by majority opinion. Highest regard is accorded to private initiative and individualism which, together with the backing of many religious groups, have been factors leading to the establishment of the strong private sector in the higher education system.

Diversity, which is the distinctive feature of the higher education system in the United States, is so broad and great that it challenges the very idea of a single system. It would be more accurate to say 50 systems exist in the United States, but in the aggregate they form a "system" reflecting the quirks and peculiarities of the country itself. And, in lesser degrees, the same may be said for the other countries in the study: each of the nationwide systems harbors variations in patterns and functions that result from its setting, the composition of the population, and the untold ingredients that nourish its evolution.

Whatever the combination of ethnic roots, traditions, customs, and religious beliefs forming a country, a cultural heritage emerges as a nation's cultural identity—which higher education systems are expected to protect and advance. This purpose for higher education, whether expressed or assumed, will be among a country's goals for its system.

ECONOMIC STAGE

The various economic stages in which countries find themselves are a further factor determining what the society wants from its system of higher education, the goals they set deliberately or unconsciously, and how much money they are willing to spend on higher education. Again, the range among the countries is exceedingly great.

Most are highly developed, industrialized nations, "postindustrialized" some would say. Japan, West Germany, and the United States lead the world in gross national product. These are technological economies supported by advanced levels of specialized research and study in universities and training in skills, production, and performance in other institutions of their higher education systems. The emphasis on specialization has often resulted in narrow training and the consequent need for more general education, related studies, and a broader focus on complex issues.

On the other hand, Mexico, Iran, and Thailand have agricultural bases for their economies and are considered developing societies. Mexico and Iran, however, possess vast resources in oil that produce rapid wealth and hasten progress toward industrialization if funds are so spent. Technological development is still a great challenge to them and their higher education systems. Training in a wide number of basic fields is required; the number and quality of teachers must be increased, and student motivation and talent encouraged.

In a more advanced stage, Poland is working toward modernization, and Australia also faces the challenge of internal technological development and building its own economy if it is not to leave the development of its rich natural resources to multinational corporations. These countries are in a position to learn much from the highly industrialized nations, especially from the mistakes made in the zealous pursuit of industrialization.

While the countries are in various developmental stages and have their individual problems, the economic scene is a global one and relates them to each other. Not only are the currencies interdependent, but severe economic dislocations, like the energy crisis, affect them simultaneously in one way or another. The highly industrialized nations, heavily dependent on energy resources, are hard hit by oil shortages and costs. And, with notable exceptions, many are suffering from high rates of inflation.

Expenditures are being reevaluated according to shifting priorities, and higher education—an item of considerable cost—is not immune in the shuffle. Allocations are being questioned and general redistribution is occurring just at the time when some higher education systems are beginning to decline in enrollment, on which their financing formulas are based. Reports from these countries in the ICED study indicate the difficult problems attending the end of the expansionary growth period. The economics of higher education systems are inevitably an integral part of the society's economic status.

POLITICAL FORM

Perhaps even more formative than economic aspects in influencing higher education systems is the political structure and stance of the government. In many countries, the higher education system is an integral branch of government—faculty are civil servants, and ministers of education are cabinet officers. In other countries, the relationship is close, if not integral, and in either case the government is the main source of financial support.

Governments—whether national, state, local, or all three—pay most, if not all, of the bills for higher education. Governments therefore generally determine the size and total budget of systems of higher education as well as their processes and methods of planning, management, and general regulations. And, in most countries, governments approve the curricula and their contents.

The extent to which governments wield their power depends largely on the political form of the society. A democracy, whether federal or unitary, will obviously bow more deeply to the autonomy of institutions of higher education than the authoritarian state. Still the areas of specific control may vary with the aims of the particular government, the wisdom of its leaders, and the temper and heritage of the people.

While the great majority of the countries in the study are democratic, three are more or less authoritarian with political power highly centralized: Iran (whether before or after the revolution of 1979), Poland, and Thailand.

Circumstances, of course, are extremely different in each of the three countries. The situation in Iran is as unstable and unpredictable as the government; Poland exhibits significant democratic traits within a Communist dominated government; and Thailand, since the coup of 1976, has not publicized its governmental practices. Nevertheless, political control in these countries is highly centralized.

Mexico is also difficult to classify for its own reasons. It is a federal democratic republic, electing its government with universal suffrage, but one party—the Institutional Revolutionary Party—has dominated the government since 1929. In effect, it is monolithic with single-party control in political matters even though its organization is federal.[8] Unitary power, held by one strong party, operates within the federal structure. The four countries that have single-party or single-person control are also the less highly developed economically of the dozen in the study.

But the inference cannot be drawn that political authoritarian power leads automatically to tightly controlled systems of higher education. It may or may not. Mexico and Iran have relatively disorganized systems but elements of close institutional control. Poland and Thailand, however, are structured with system-wide supervision that includes clearly delineated organizational channels for operations and approval.

The other nations are in the democratic mode with multi-party control. They vary primarily in organization of political power—whether it is federal or unitary. Australia, Canada, the Federal Republic of Germany, and the United States are federal forms of government with states or provinces having considerable powers, especially over their higher education systems.

In the alternative category of unitary form are France, Japan, Sweden, and the United Kingdom (with elements of federalism controlling higher education). Political power is basically centralized, and their higher education systems generally reflect this aspect.

Certainly the political posture of the government and its organization are key factors in establishing the basic structure of the system of higher education and in setting its operations. But it must be increasingly apparent that exceptions and qualifications constantly challenge grouping the countries and their higher education systems in this or that category. Neat and logical schemes quickly reveal their arbitrary nature just as stereotypes seldom exist.

Beneath the rather gross assignments to general types lie answers to important questions that concern operations of the systems and point to the directions in which they are moving:

How powerful are the states or provinces in the federal organizations? Do they have
   primary, constitutional responsibility for higher education? Are they exercising
   their responsibility?

Where is the prime source of funds for the higher education system? Who makes the
    final decision on expenditures?
Regardless of federal organization, is the trend in the country toward power in the
    central government?
If the country is unitary in organization and centralized, is the effort toward
    decentralization of control and participation?

Answers to such questions are the intent of this study as it describes what is
happening in higher education systems in the 12 countries.

    This initial discussion of the setting may serve better in illuminating
differences than proving similarities. If so, it is valuable. Even a brief
recognition of the basic elements—the physical, social, economic, and
political factors—that comprise the milieu from which higher education
systems arise provides a reminder of the environment in which the systems
function. It helps explain some of the problems they face, and especially the
different solutions they are trying.

2
NATIONAL GOALS

Regardless of the wide diversity among the various countries in our study, their current statements of goals for their higher education systems are remarkably similar. In this they conform far more than in other comparative aspects. Perhaps the limits of rhetoric and word choice, or simply the limits of imagination, restrict statements of goals and result in common expressions. Or maybe the similarity of tasks performed in higher institutions promotes the use of corresponding phrases. In any case, the expectations of nations for their higher education systems vary little.

But significant variations do appear in the priority of goals—where the emphasis is placed among several aims. In the priority assigned to a goal, countries give evidence of their economic concerns, political climate, and social aspirations.

Some who participated in the study, however, question the value of goals themselves. Clark Kerr asks if they are really necessary and suggests they can be divisive, and even a menace. Warning against the pitfalls in setting up goals, he argues, in part, for the incremental approach in the budgetary process, which allows adjustments for change or reaffirmation of goals.[1] The incremental approach is a short-range, pragmatic approach that is adaptable in a pluralistic society with many goals like the United States. But it does not require a basic reconsideration of purposes or goals; it is more likely to juggle items up or down without fundamentally questioning the purpose.

Moreover, the incremental budget process is coming upon hard times. Because of financial cutbacks, the process is more often decremental, with across the board decreases, or particular areas are targeted for increase according to perceived needs of society, while the rest of the items remain in a "steady-state." Choosing the area for cuts is a negative expression of goals; what is not cut presumably is most necessary or valuable.

Tony Becher in the British report suggests critically that "the very talk of goals and objectives is misleadingly teleological." Too many heterogeneous people comprise the different types of institutions that, at best, are a loose federation of subject departments—hardly the best set-up for agreement on common policy, much less the definition of goals. He concludes that when assessment of higher education is sought, it is better to consider *functions*— what the system is generally called upon to do.[2]

Becher's separation of functions and goals is useful. The same distinction is recommended by Jan Szczepański in the Polish report and is adopted here.[3] In this discussion, goals and purposes are equated, meaning the ideal, the overall objective, the desired effects on a nationwide scale. They are thus in contrast to the ways and means of effecting the desired results which are the functions of the system or the tasks it performs. Functions are more specific in results and generally more important as determinants of the total consequences to the society than the rhetoric of goals.

However, the present text is also admittedly idealistic in upholding statements of goals which can help to unify and guide the general development of higher education systems. Goals need be neither divisive nor unrealistic. Goals are slippery, difficult to define and interpret, and are notoriously hard to attain. But without at least the rhetoric of direction and objectives, systems of higher education become headless horsemen galloping away in all directions at once. It is a too frequent spectacle in higher education.

To be sure, there are unstated goals and functions that may be latent or simply understood and assumed. Higher education has been around a long time and its existence taken for granted. Some functions have developed that were not intentional. Such an unseen benefit is the caretaker function. Some call it the "parking lot" or "baby-sitting" service for society. Higher institutions perform a holding operation for young people to prevent a deluge in the labor market, which is unprepared to offer sufficient opportunities for employment. While the ostensible purpose is giving advanced training to those motivated and able, mass enrollments make it inevitably a period of waiting for others.

Since higher education traditionally has coincided with the years of reaching social and biological maturation in the human life cycle, it has assumed functions suitable to these developmental years that can scarcely be classified as academic education. To encompass these needs, the definition of education has broadened to include the whole person. Society has gradually added to the assignments for higher education, asking it to pick up functions that once were the responsibilities of families, churches, and other social institutions. Many of these functions are assumed and remain unstated goals. Such additional responsibilities have been recognized only in part by higher education systems in most countries, but in the United States they are widely accepted. The United States is atypical in this function as it is in many aspects of its higher education.

Attention here concentrates on statements drawn from both official and informal sources by authors of the 12 country reports. After a review of the sources used for the various countries, national goals are discussed and priorities indicated.

Thailand and Mexico turn first to the charters establishing individual institutions. Thailand adds specific statements from its National Economic and Social Development Plans; and Mexico quotes from the National Association of Universities and Insititutions of Higher Education, a voluntary group which serves as the main forum and spokesman for higher education. Iran (before the revolution) depended primarily on a report from the Plan and Budget Organization of the government.

Canada, the United Kingdom, Australia, and the United States take words from distinguished ad hoc commissions representing national interests, and from ministers of government.

The other countries have official statements from laws duly enacted. Nationally legislated goals come from Poland, Sweden, France, Japan, and West Germany. The more highly organized and centralist countries and those with planned economies are naturally more apt to have formal and generally inclusive statements. But it is of interest to note that federally organized West Germany has joined the centralist group in this respect.

More national statements on goals and more legislated functions can be expected, even in the more loosely organized countries, as the government role expands with funding of higher education. In the past it was rare to have such public statements, but recently they have appeared with increasing frequency. And, once the government gets into the act, it is not apt to leave the stage. Seldom do governments discontinue or decrease their involvement in an established area, and statements of expectations are bound to accompany allotments. The policy of "no strings attached" is on its way out.

Rune Premfors gives some chronology on the appearance of public statements concerning policy goals in Sweden. Comprehensive objectives were not issued by the government until 1959 in the planning report of the "U55" commission. Before then statements were specific on subjects like the training of medical doctors. After U55, national policy goals were increasingly stated in subsequent commission reports, government bills, and other documents for higher education.[4] These have culminated in the "U68" report and in detailed legislation that has followed and is now being implemented.

France expressed national goals for higher education in its Orientation Law of the same year—1968. West Germany's Frame Law passed in 1976; and Australia's Commonwealth Parliament, in 1977, created the new Tertiary Education Commission, broadening the definition of higher education to include technical and further training, signalling a shift in public policy to expand and encourage technical training. Earlier and under very different circumstances, Poland's government legislated goals for the higher education system in 1958, and Japan had enacted the School Education Law in 1947.

Examination of national goals reveals three overarching interests and the following general order of priority. Higher education systems are asked to contribute to:

(1) Economic progress
(2) Equality and democratization
(3) Social betterment

The categories are large enough and sufficiently embracing to support the claim of similarities among the countries' goals. They are, moreover, broad enough to cover the detailed differences in semantics and the variations in functions specified by the countries for their achievement. Differing priorities for individual countries are noted in the text on the particular objective.

ECONOMIC PROGRESS

Manpower requirements are recurring words high on lists of national goals for higher education systems. The favorable correlation between economic growth and higher levels of education has not escaped the notice of governments, although research of late questions the positive relationship long accepted. Whatever the stage of economic development, governments maintain the view that providing manpower for society's economic progress is a major purpose of advanced learning.

Agriculturally based economies in the developing countries naturally have the heaviest and broadest demands for trained personnel in all fields— elementary and specialized. Technologically advanced nations, on the other hand, have more specific needs that shift more rapidly among fields. Their problems are to uphold industrialized society, to push forward its advancement, and to find solutions to the new problems created by industrialization. Research and training in higher education centers are thus vital to both the developing and advanced nations. The focus and spread are simply different in the two stages, and the handicaps encountered are very different.

Problems in meeting the goal for manpower needs in developing countries are extreme and basic. Reports from Mexico and Iran emphasize the essential need for adequate faculty in both numbers and qualifications before goals can be approached. Mexico, for example, has an excessive number of part-time faculty: only 11.7 percent of the approximate total of 47,000 faculty in higher education institutions are full-time. The great majority are part-time, not even half-time.[5]

To approach any of the goals expressed requires basic change in the attitude toward teaching and provision for committed, well-prepared faculty. Recognizing the situation, Mexico's objectives stress the preparation of faculty members and researchers, particularly in fields directly related to socioeconomic development, both regional and national. The goal is to improve the standard of living, and work toward the solution of society's problems through the application of scientific knowledge.

Iran, too, faces serious widespread shortages of qualified teachers while many professors have been supplementing their income by serving in government posts. At the same time, there are overwhelming demands for trained manpower. A government study conducted in 1970 estimated that, by 1978, the country needed 2,990 percent more secondary school teachers, 1,122 percent more general engineers, 660 percent more chemical technicians, and so forth. The conclusion was simply that it was impossible. It is doubly discouraging when meeting manpower needs "constitutes the single most important task of higher education in Iran."[6]

The authors comment further that in its present stage of economic growth "Iran cannot afford to pursue a policy of liberal arts or education for education's sake." The needs and potential for economic development should be a decisive factor in determining the direction of a university's activity.

Thailand's report places the same goal first: training manpower. The last two national plans called especially for high-level manpower in engineering, agriculture, medicine, and sciences, and the current plan continues the emphasis by stressing "education in the fields required by market demand and necessary for national development."[7]

During the period of reconstruction in Poland, which was truly remarkable, the Sejm passed the Higher Education Act officially proclaiming two paramount goals for the higher education system:

1. Instruction of qualified personnel for all jobs in the economy, culture, and all sectors of social life requiring credentials from higher education.
2. Education of scientific manpower for all research and development institutions, and education of academic teachers.[8]

Today, in the next stage of development referred to as "modernization," Poland's goals remain unchanged. Manpower orientation is the first purpose of higher education, although it assumes a general education base and philosophic outlook embracing Marxist theory.

One may expect countries to push the economic goal above all others when they strive for entry into industrialized status, but once there, it would seem that other aims like individual fulfillment and concern for the quality of life should at least broaden the purely practical purposes for higher education. Such, however, is not the case generally from the national viewpoint. Economic progress continues to dominate in highly developed economies, and it is quite unrelated to the political stance of a nation, which appears later in the methods adopted to achieve the goal.

The Australian report names manpower as the first goal in its several objectives for higher education, and the United Kingdom states, from the Robbins' Report in 1963, that the first objective is the "instruction in skills suitable to play a part in the general division of labor."[9]

Jack Embling, the author of this part of the United Kingdom report, is careful to give context, pointing out that this goal is one of four objectives essential in "any properly balanced system." He suggests the Robbins' Committee put the economic goal first, not because of its relative importance, "but as a realistic assessment of what most students have in mind in undertaking higher education, i.e., what will enhance their careers and increase their income."

And Embling goes on to say that though the first objective was utilitarian, the method to attain it was "to promote the general powers of the mind." Career training, "even where it is concerned with practical techniques, should be on a plane of generality that makes possible their application to many problems." There is evidence of academic discomfort with the emphasis on the practical, economic purpose for higher training. But, according to the position held by most countries, the Robbins' Committee was on target in its assessment of national aims.

The federal government of Canada has picked out this goal as a primary concern on the national level. Although the provinces have constitutional responsibility for higher education, the Prime Minister, in 1966, drew a line of demarcation on this point:

> Education is obviously a matter of profound importance to the economic and social growth of the country as a whole. This is particularly true of higher education.... The federal government accepts primary responsibility for employment and economic activity generally in the country.... The preparation of our young people for productive participation in the labor force of the country is a matter of vital concern to all Canadians.[10]

Later, he specifically claimed federal jurisdiction over adult occupational training as part of the responsibility for national economic development.

Japan's actual record toward the goal of economic progress speaks for itself. As a goal for higher education, it was not mentioned in the Education Law of 1946 promulgated by the U.S. occupation. But, early in the 1950s, "powerful financial corporations lobbied for educational policies that would provide needed manpower to meet the economic growth."[11] The Japan Federation of Business Managers submitted a *Suggestion for Reform of the*

Educational System that called for diversification of upper secondary and higher educational systems and immediate expansion in science and technology.

Over the ensuing years, until 1963, the Ministry of Education was confronted with plans from the Department of Economic Planning, the Economic Council (estimating a shortage of 170,000 scientists and technologists), and the Council on Scientific and Technological Affairs. The Ministry's plans and estimates appear to have been consistently conservative and cautious, planning an increase of only 16,000 over approximately seven years beginning in 1961. "The industrial sector was not satisfied with such a compromise."

Adjustments occurred, procedures to establish new scientific and technological departments were eased, and private institutions admitted more students than anticipated. By 1963, there were approximately 100,000 graduates in science and technology. A new junior college level technical course was started during this period: the five-year higher technical school which followed the basic nine-year compulsory program. Not many of the other countries' education ministries would probably welcome such pressure from the economic and technological communities, but the coordinated effort in Japan was spectacular in results if judged by Japan's position today in the world's trade and money markets.

The United States experience was also dramatic in the late fifties after the success of Sputnik. On recommendation from two ad hoc commissions, one a President's commission and the other representing a private foundation, the government mounted a drive with federal funds to increase capability in science and technology suitable for the space age. Although national security interests were clearly a factor, economic progress was equally served.

Manpower objectives, however, have not been an undisputed goal for higher education in the United States, and they have not received first priority. More than the undependability of statistical prediction, there is fundamental controversy over government planning and individual choice. The argument is perhaps even greater in the United States than in the other democratic countries participating in the study.

Nevertheless, the United States joins all the other countries' concern for economic progress in the present emphasis on vocational, career, and professional preparation. Higher education is increasingly expected to be practical. It is like a tidal wave around the world. Practical application, work-study combinations, experience beyond the classroom—every country uses such language and registers its current disenchantment with the theoretical and speculative scholarship of the ivory tower tradition.

Sweden is unequivocal and forthright—beyond other countries—in asserting "that *all* higher education should aim at teaching students some kind of vocational skill."[12] Few are so explicit in stressing vocational orientation in curricula. The goal of economic welfare is challenged only by social equality in Sweden, and cultural goals receive correspondingly less emphasis.

Even West Germany's strong research orientation which, according to Humboldt's dictum, was to be "free of immediate social concerns," has been modified by the 1976 Frame Law:

> All areas of science as well as the practical application of scientific knowledge including the consequences that may follow its application, can be the subject of research at institutions of higher education, depending on the particular nature of an individual institution. (Art. 22.)[13]

Higher education's purpose is to prepare students for professional fields. Regulations emphasize practical experience so that studies and research are "aimed more toward professional and social demand."

Throughout the countries of the study, the national goal for higher education to further economic progress has expressed itself not only in concern for manpower requirements: it has energized the push toward vocational training, career preparation, and the practical, applied aspects of both the curriculum and research.

Economic goals have long existed for higher learning on the latent level, and sometimes they have been openly manifest at decisive turning points for higher education systems. For example, the well-known Land Grant College Act in the mid nineteenth century in the United States, which sponsored training for agriculture and industrial development, had its origins in economic goals. Diversity in programs, like technical, managerial, and industrial training courses, is the result of the thrust toward economic progress. Such courses constitute the expanding front of curricula in higher education and are evidence of the system's adjustment to the needs of society.

EQUALITY AND DEMOCRATIZATION

If economic progress has fathered diversity in higher education programs, the national goal of equality of opportunity has fostered growth in the size of systems and diversity in the student body. Further, equality as a goal for higher education systems is relatively recent in origin. Systems were frankly elitist, and growth was gradual until after World War II, when growth spread into a mass movement.

Governments, regardless of political persuasion and organizational structure, rather quickly adopted the goal of equality. In an era attuned to social justice, equality of opportunity for higher education is a powerful political tool as well as a means toward the goal itself. The phenomenon is worldwide: it has happened in every country in the study—democratic, socialist, communist and authoritarian.

Social equality as a goal for higher education has dominated Sweden more than other Western countries, although it did not become official rhetoric until the late 1960s. Since then, according to Rune Premfors, it has been deemphasized somewhat, alternating with economic welfare for prime position, but it remains very important among policy goals for higher education, even for the new nonsocialist government.[14]

The United States report gives the goal of equality first priority, and no country fails to place it high on the list. In a broad sense, equality is pervasive and assumed as goals include development of individuals and general contributions to society.

But governments have not taken this for granted. They have encouraged and pushed expansion of opportunities, poured large sums of money into higher education systems, increased financial assistance to students, and some have gone so far as quota formulas to aid the disadvantaged and to protect equality of opportunity. These efforts are discussed in detail in Chapter 7.

In this instance, the national goal of equality of opportunity for higher education stands on its achievement record. It is, by all odds, the most spectacular development of the last three decades, and the achievement has brought with it the greatest changes and problems. The closed society of the elite led by the chaired professor has been surrounded and invaded by consumer demand supported by government. Revolutionary terms are applicable to the mass movement in many countries that has captured the attention and consumed the energies of this generation of educators. The vast expansion of higher education and democratization of its structure have led to the formation of systems of higher education as a means of control, of maintaining order in the face of tremendous growth.

Comparison of figures before and after to show the extraordinary growth in higher education systems in the last thirty years does not tell the full story because the basic definition of higher education has expanded. It is no longer limited to colleges, universities, and professional schools; higher education now generally encompasses teachers colleges, technical institutes, and shorter programs of junior and community colleges, as in Japan, the United States, and Canada.

An exception is Poland where the higher education establishment has held against the inclusion and even the introduction of community-college type programs. An experiment with a three-year *studium* lasted only a few years since such short programs "could not properly introduce students to the rigors of scientific research." Hence they could not be considered higher education, and "there was no place for the graduates of such schools in the hierarchy of posts in the economy."[15]

Poland's hard line against the community-college-type of higher education is atypical compared to the other nations and odd, especially in view of the extensive array of other types of institutions in the contemporary Polish system. Beyond universities and polytechnics, the present system comprises agricultural, economic, and medical academies, colleges of pedagogy, social science, fine arts, music, theatre and film, naval studies, gymnastics and sports, and two theological academies.[16]

Even the rather rigid and traditional definition of universities as *the* higher education in West Germany has given way to include teachers colleges, *Fachhochschulen* (former engineering and advanced vocational schools) with three-year courses more oriented to practice, and the 11 new comprehensive universities formed partly by combining existing institutions. All together they comprise the present higher education system.[17]

Besides broadening the concept of what constitutes higher education, the goal of equal opportunity is dramatically affecting the student constituency. Student bodies are not only much larger, there are many more women, and more socioeconomic and ethnic groups represented. Above all, there are very different age groups entering higher education and changing study patterns. A remarkable increase is occurring in older students, employed persons, and part-time students. Sweden, the United States, and Poland lead in this development in what undoubtedly is a most significant trend.

Forty percent of all students in Poland's system in 1978 were employed persons.[18] Sweden's system has steadily increased in the number of new entrants 25 years old and over from 17 percent in 1968 to more than 62 percent in 1975.[19]

In the United States, over the years 1972–78, the percentage of persons age 25 and over enrolled in higher education rose from 28 to 34.8 percent, which represented some 4 million people.[20] Of these, two out of three generally would be part-time students. The figures for participation in *adult education*, including noncollegiate postsecondary programs, proprietary schools, and other institutions with formal instruction, are of course much higher, and harder to count. Estimates for total participants in 1978 were in the neighborhood of 20 million, but this embraces many categories not considered in the higher education system.

At the same time that older people are taking advantage of educational opportunities, the numbers of students in the usual age group (18- to 21- or 24-year-olds, depending on the country), have multiplied many times. Participation rates from the age cohort over a period of years give a fairly accurate picture of the expansion within a country, and percentages allow a rough comparison among the countries.

In France, the participation rate (percentage of population 19 to 23 years) in higher education has grown from 7.7 percent in 1960 to 19.8 percent in 1976.[21] Australia has comparably moved from 10.7 percent (in

1968) enrolled in universities and colleges of advanced education to 19.1 percent in 1976.[22] Canada reached a national average of 20 percent in 1975–76.[23]

In terms of *new entrants* in universities, junior colleges and higher technical schools, the numbers in Japan increased to 38.3 percent of the total college-age group by 1975. Japanese secondary school graduates grew from 27 to 49 percent of the age group between 1951 and 1975; and applicants to higher education increased accordingly, which partially accounts for the intense competition in admissions.[24]

New entrants have been rising steadily in France since 1969–70, and predictions indicate a long-term trend.[25] West Germany, too, has continued to climb rapidly in student numbers in the 1970s, in contrast to countries where high expansion rates have slowed down or shifted.[26] Sweden, for example, reached its enrollment peak in 1970, then declined for four years until 1975 when the curve turned upward again.[27]

With variations in growth rates, the 12 countries' higher education systems have responded remarkably to the demand for equality of opportunity. Gross figures alone show the magnitude of the impact. Total size in enrollment has multiplied five and six times in many countries. It has more than doubled in every country. Although some started with the influx of veterans after World War II, all the systems joined the movement which expanded most in the sixties, supported economically by the affluence of people and the governments. After that, the story begins to vary in different countries.

Achievement toward the goal of equal educational opportunity can be measured more easily than progress toward other goals for higher education. Enrollment numbers show the progress and categories clarify the effects on subgroups of the population by age, sex, race, and economic background. Nevertheless, other national goals like economic progress and social advancement are inevitably intertwined in the motivation of both public policy and the people.

People's aspirations have risen and higher education's limits are disappearing, except physically in the actual number of places for students. Education is conceived as continuing, life-long, *permanente*, and universal. Among the countries in our study, only the Federal Republic of Germany has actually declared higher education a *civil right*, but all assume it to be and act accordingly.

While the achievement record is admirable, social demand continues and is stimulated by population growth in many countries. Mexico's enrollment was still increasing at the annual rate of 18 percent in 1978.[28] And, regardless of an enrollment increase by six times in Iran between 1961 and 1975, government universities could accept only 10 percent of the total number of applicants in the latter year.[29] Of the more highly developed countries, West Germany has the most severe backlog of applicants awaiting entrance.

Australia's self-assessment recognizes that even though progress toward equality of opportunity has been considerable, "children from families in the lower income groups are underrepresented significantly in tertiary education."[30] The United States still pursues its efforts to assist minorities. Edward Sheffield from Canada reports that results there are rather discouraging. Wide inequality remains in participation, especially among the provinces, and postsecondary opportunities for working adults are inadequate.[31] Pursuit of equality in opportunities for higher education is a long, endless process.

Regional development of systems has accompanied expansion in order to provide access geographically for potential students. Communication media are increasingly employed to overcome handicaps in location and extend opportunities to new groups. The changes brought by efforts to equalize opportunity are extremely fundamental as well as far-reaching in effects on higher learning. The general result, outside of authoritarian countries, is a democratization of the entire system: its student constituency, faculty, administrative and organizational structure.

SOCIAL BETTERMENT

Social goals for higher education systems spread out over an even larger spectrum than the other two interrelated areas of economic progress and equality of opportunity. Overlap is apparent among the three and especially so in the broadly defined social aspects. Thus the differences in countries' statements are greater, both in the importance given to certain functions and in the range of concern.

Reasons for the social goals selected often appear in the problems the country is facing. And, of course, singling out a particular function for higher education reveals the value structure of the society at a certain period of time. An example is the position awarded to the preservation and advancement of the cultural heritage of a society. Each country would implicitly hold this goal for its higher education system, but just five of the countries see fit to express it with emphasis: Poland, Thailand, Mexico, Canada, and the United Kingdom.

Perhaps the others assume that cultural inheritance is maintained by a process of osmosis in the society or that national pride and understanding are instilled at the secondary level where textbooks on a country's history are customarily included. In some instances, such texts are required on the tertiary level—attesting to the goal—but it is simply omitted in national policy statements. All would surely agree on the merits of the goal; only most do not overtly call attention to it as a major responsibility for the system of higher education.

Poland's deep concern for its cultural heritage is a basic matter of identity for people who have been their own master for a tragically short period in modern history. Their report to the ICED study makes this fact abundantly clear in the text, although the goal is listed fifth out of seven official purposes set by law. Events in their political life have threatened the sense of identity and heightened the concern.

Higher education has gone underground periodically since the late nineteenth century and, starting in 1978, a "flying university" surfaced in which professors meet with students in various parts of the country. One purpose claimed is to teach subjects not otherwise included in the curriculum; another beyond doubt is the reassertion of Polish cultural identity. The movement is sufficiently challenging to have received official reaction and the imposition of restraints.[32]

Thailand unequivocally asserts the goal. Cultural preservation is specifically stated in the laws establishing every university since the Chulalongkorn University Act in 1943 with one exception—the National Institute of Development Administration.[33] There is no question about its prominence.

Cultural development and national unity are two outstanding goals drawn from a number of federal objectives by the Canadian report. The first recognizes the threat posed to Canadian culture by the United States and the fact that "Canadians still seek identity." The second purpose, national unity, is a goal because of tension and inequalities among the regions, and, in particular, Quebec's efforts to secede from the federation of provinces.[34] Although secession has not occurred, the problems remain deep and divisive.

Britain affirms the transmission of a common culture as a fundamental purpose of higher education, but in a somewhat broader context that is admittedly difficult to define in concise terms. Like other national purposes, it was first stated by the Robbins' Committee and elaborated briefly to include the transmission of "common standards of citizenship." Jack Embling explains, with a further quotation, that "it did not mean forcing all individuality into a common mould, but 'providing in partnership with the family that background of culture and social habit upon which a healthy society depends.' "[35] Although the Committee's statement "seems to imply conformity to an ethos to which the individual is subordinated," such was not the intent, and individual development is both obvious and implicit in other objectives and as a matter of fact.

Social goals are even broader, more diffuse, and pervasive in Mexico than in the other countries mentioned thus far. A summary of purposes assigned to universities by their governing laws includes repeated reference to furthering "social cohesion," "cultural independence," "cultural...and social development of the states," "human solidarity," and "human coexistence." Objectives coalesce on social responsibility, problem-solving, and service to the development of the country "in a context of social justice and freedom."[36]

The political component is pronounced in some statements concerning social objectives for higher education systems. Poland specifically asks for "political and civic education" and "preparation of the student for political activity,"[37] which means ideological instruction for participation in the Marxist society. West Germany requests that teaching and studies prepare the student not only professionally, but also "to act responsibly in a liberal, democratic, social, and constitutional state."[38] Sweden's planning goals include one aimed at democracy, explaining that although this is a task mainly for compulsory education, "higher education should aim to foster the cooperative and critical spirits that a democracy needs, and be careful not to educate narrow experts."[39]

Higher education's role as critic of its society—the gadfly function of Socrates—is reaffirmed by several countries besides Sweden. Universities and other institutions of higher education in Mexico see the critic's role as an exercise of academic freedom in pointing out errors and proposing solutions for national problems.[40]

Australia's report comments:

One of the roles of a university in a free society is to be the conscience and critic of that society; such a role cannot be fulfilled if the university is expected to be the arm of government policy.[41]

Scholars and scientists who spend their lives in the search for knowledge and truth should, at least in their own spheres of inquiry, "be proof against the waves of emotion and prejudice which make the ordinary man, and public opinion, subject from time to time to illusion and self-deceit." The author, Bruce Williams, concludes that these are proud objectives and when lived up to they render great public service.

In the United States, too, higher education is expected to serve social criticism. Without it, there can be neither effective adjustment nor advancement in the society. Faculty and students are expected to make this contribution, though it is not always welcomed by the society at large. Viewing the improvement of society as the single most important function of higher education, the Truman Commission, some 30 years ago, urged that higher institutions serve as an instrument of social transition, defining their goal as the kind of civilization society hopes to build. Those who formulate policies and programs "must have a vision of the nation and the world we want."[42]

Under the broad panoply of social values, which higher education is to foster, the nations generally include moral and ethical behavior. More than acting responsibly, as West Germany puts it, or the general focus on constructive uses of knowledge in Mexico's goals, Japan asks for "moral character." Thailand emphasizes the contribution of a worthwhile life to society. Higher education is "to serve man and society so that mankind may live contentedly in harmony with nature."[43]

Sweden's U68 report stresses values; the United States speaks for enduring human values, and the ethical development of students; and the charter of Australia's University of Sydney calls for the "better advancement of religion and morality."[44] No doubt, if the charters of older institutions in the various countries were searched, such declarations would be more frequent. Religious foundations were a main motivating force for establishment. Thus, although economic development appears as the overriding concern among national goals, idealistic hopes for the improvement of man and a better world are not totally forgotten.

The concept of public service as a function for higher institutions takes a different configuration in the line-up of nations, depending upon how it is understood. All subscribe to it in the broadest interpretation of service to society by graduates. Teaching and research are a public service by their very nature. So Australia's report concludes that universities render a public service simply in being themselves.[45] It is not assumed that they should also serve their immediate communities in active, direct programs.

With this position, the majority of countries agree. British, French, or West German universities are hardly expected to go to work on housing, health, or any other social program for their neighborhoods or cities. Faculty may be advisors and students may work practically in conjunction with their studies, but institutions do not sponsor, much less lead, in community development.

The United States' acceptance of practical responsibility on the part of higher learning institutions for their communities in basic, physical aspects is unique among nations. The United States tradition is highly pragmatic and extends well beyond serving government with expertise in consulting capacities or appointments that would be typical of many other countries. It is not merely a matter of degree of difference, it is the type of activity expected.

In the summer of 1978, presidents of 50 urban universities, evenly divided between public and private institutions, met in Washington, D. C., and pledged active support for the President's urban policy to revitalize decaying cities. They accepted responsibility as appropriate institutions to activate renewal at the local level through programs that involved faculty training to work on crime prevention, medical services, job creation, and so on.

That kind of action from universities could not be imagined in most parts of the world. Among other countries, Poland is most similar to the United States to the extent that its Higher Education Act says that all institutions of higher education are to "render services for the communities where the institutions are located."[46] The injunction is not interpreted in the Polish text aside from comment on courses given in various locales, which would characterize many countries' concepts of public service.

The U. K. report calls attention to the American concept of service to society and points to the difference in British attitude. But, it is noted that government officials have spoken about the desirability of having a substantial part of the higher education system under social control and "directly responsive to social needs." The polytechnics were conceived to be "rooted in their regions and localities." The author suggests that though this "intimate relationship between institution and community has never been spelled out, the hints given indicate an edging towards the American concept."[47]

It would be very surprising indeed if the public service role for systems of higher education did not receive increasingly greater pressure from societies and governments. The thrust accompanies equality and democratization, it goes with more participation from interest groups in the society, and government's need to use higher education systems to further public goals.

Other countries may well move in the direction already taken by the United States. Reexamination of objectives for systems invites additional functions and specificity as public policy tries to measure results. Universities will be the segment of higher education systems most directly affected, since technical institutions and two- or three-year institutes and colleges are usually more closely allied to local interests.

INTERNATIONALISM

A study covering 12 countries like this one cannot fail to consider internationalism as a function of higher education even though it receives scant attention in country reports. Its importance to the future of interrelated countries stands without question, yet it has not been prominent in the expressed concerns of governments or societies.

Sweden alone really stresses international dimensions as part of higher education's responsibilities. First advanced as a goal in the U68 report, the idea that a truly global perspective, emphasizing the needs of Third World countries, should pervade higher education lasted through several drafts and made its way into the Higher Education Act. The goal was to increase understanding and knowledge, through research and teaching, about other countries and international conditions.[48] Evidence suggests Sweden actively pursues the goal.

On a somewhat different basis, Canada, too, claims internationalism as an objective and names it among six priorities. It is an area for which the federal government asserts special concern: higher education is to assume "appropriate international responsibilities." The interpretation, however, limits the concept. According to Sheffield's evaluation, international responsibilities mean external aid programs, which seem to be effective, and Canada's anxiety about numbers of foreign faculty and students. Internationalism is not discussed in terms of influencing teaching content and attention to global issues.[49]

Two countries, France and West Germany, mention international aspects in their higher education laws, but their reports in the study do not comment on this as either a goal or function. Both nations' laws reflect the European common market policy for cooperation. The French Orientation Law, for example, says that special relations shall be established with universities of the member states, and adds that higher institutions shall initiate and develop international cooperation "especially with universities that are wholly or partly French-speaking."[50]

The Framework Law of West Germany similarly reminds universities and colleges that they are:

> ...to promote international and, in particular, European cooperation and exchange between German and foreign universities and colleges; they are also to take the particular requirements of foreign students into consideration.[51]

It is not suggested that other countries omitting mention of internationalism are completely ignoring it in their higher education systems. Nonetheless, this important area is not getting the attention it should: the general neglect is dangerous to world understanding and prejudices national action through ignorance.

Country awareness gives signs of increasing, but action to amend the situation is inadequate and long overdue. In 1978, Britain inaugurated a five-year plan to emphasize Third World issues in teacher training and other less orthodox ways. The action followed a survey that revealed "two-thirds of the nation holds parochial and introverted views and is unsympathetic to a world perspective."[52]

In the same year, the President of the United States appointed a Commission on Foreign Language and International Studies under the chairmanship of James A. Perkins, because "the U. S. educational system is woefully deficient in preparing Americans to live in a highly interdependent world." The Commission's recommendations have been made; they are intelligent and bold in scope. Funding is another matter, and skeptics recall that no federal funds have ever been appropriated for the International Educational Act passed in 1966 as part of President Johnson's "Great Society" program.[53]

The record is not encouraging in any of our countries except Sweden and, to a lesser extent, Canada. Still, students are moving ahead in exchange programs and studies abroad, faculty are extending foreign contacts steadily in professional associations that are international, and communication media are bridging many gaps in knowledge left vacant by higher education programs.

OTHER RELATED GOALS

Throughout the discussion of goals the fundamental purpose of individual development and fulfillment has been more or less taken for granted. It is implicit in all education and integral to other goals. Some countries explicitly state it, and there is a difference in its importance, of course, to countries holding different political beliefs like the United States and Poland.

The United States unhesitatingly places it high on the list, while the Polish report relegates self-fulfillment next to the last position and explains that this aim is linked with political and civic education and participation in the cultural life of society. Following Marxist theory, "man can only achieve his fulfillment and the development of his personality through social interaction and cultural activity .... The general educational ideal is to produce a man who achieves his own fulfillment by serving society."[54]

While the placement and interpretation of the objective may be indicative of a society's value system at a particular time in history, it is also in many instances an implicit function assumed when knowledge, training, and skills are mentioned and when equality of opportunity is emphasized. Goals are too interrelated in higher education to permit neat separation and precise placement in a hierarchy of values.

If institutional views of goals were examined, instead of those of national systems of higher education, another set of functions would appear, especially teaching and research. If the goals of parents or of students for their own higher education were considered, still other words and emphases would be used.

From the national point of view, however, there is general agreement on the three larger categories of goals: economic progress, equality and democratization, and social betterment. If judgement of performance toward the goals has appeared harsh in some cases, it must be remembered that the potential is very great and also very important. Given the size and scope of the goals expressed by nations, higher education systems would seem to be doing a relatively adequate job. Or one could say they are doing remarkably well considering the magnitude of tasks assigned. But they could be doing very much better.

3
GOVERNMENT AND FUNDING

In examining organizational forms and administrative aspects, complications increase with the number and levels of government involved and how they, in turn, relate to the system of higher education. It is necessary to distinguish among levels of government—national, state or provincial, and local—in order to see relationships that affect the whole system as well as its sectors or parts.

Further, the levels are essential when considering the role of government and the location of power. Financial aspects—the sources of funds and the allocation process—lead to the main decision-making centers. They are the threads followed in this discussion through several parts of the structure of higher education systems. The basic autonomy of systems is therefore in question.

One caveat is in order: the location of power in government is not, *ipso facto*, bad. There is too much evidence to the contrary. No one claims that the British government has removed the autonomy of universities. The same can be said generally for most democratic governments. Nevertheless, it is of utmost importance to point out that great powers are concentrating increasingly in government, and that government itself is not always aware of this and often not cognizant of the effects of its actions on the higher education it seeks to nourish. With this in mind, the power of government as the main source of funds is considered.

Higher education systems, in overall structure, mirror the political form of their countries. In federally organized nations, the states or provinces usually play strong roles and frequently have primary responsibility for the system within their borders. In unitary countries, the central, national government has the first position of power and responsibility, which is located in one or more central ministries. The majority of our higher education systems follow the unitary government pattern, but, as always, with the ever-present and infinite variations of their own heritage, custom, and circumstance. Those variations, of course, also exist within the ranks of the federally organized systems.

Within the two general patterns of organization, every higher education system in the study has several sectors differentiated by the type and level of education offered. Most often technical and technological training in higher and lower levels forms a separate sector or two; generally teacher training has had a distinct sector, two-year colleges another, and universities have been traditionally the oldest and most distinguished sector. The complexity of the system grows in direct proportion to the number of different sectors, especially as each has its own structure of power and procedure.

One other element also must be reckoned with in an overall view of systems: namely, whether there is a private sector of higher education as well as the more standard public pattern. Four countries, two federal and two central and unitary in organization, have private higher education of any appreciable importance at the present time. After looking at the private sector, the discussion will center on the public patterns which are preeminent in higher education systems.

THE PRIVATE SECTOR

Historically, in many countries, private and religious initiative has started institutions, but gradually over the years private institutions have joined the public sector. The story has repeated itself with few exceptions. Today, in most of our countries, there are merely a handful of institutions that have survived privately, such as the College of Business Administration in Stockholm, and the Roman Catholic University in Lublin. The preponderant number of higher education systems around the world are public, governmental responsibilities. Nonetheless, exceptions exist, particularly in the United States and Japan, that are important in the context of government control and governance.

Many would claim that the existence of a private sector, especially if it is large or powerful, is a hedge against undue governmental dominance. It enjoys another source of funding which automatically underpins its independence. Operating on individual charters, private institutions may determine their own governance under the control of their own board of trustees which is frequently self-perpetuating. Furthermore, in curricular programs the private sector can provide diversity and widened choice in a pluralistic system like that in the United States, which has proved to be exceedingly effective.

The questions raised concern observable trends in the countries having a private sector: does it affect the role of government and its use of power? Or do private institutions actually maintain their autonomous status more successfully than publicly supported institutions? Is the line between private and public sectors blurring?

In our sample, only Thailand, Mexico, Japan and the United States have private higher education in any significant amount today. France might be included with this group since it has a little over 6 percent of total enrollments in private institutions. It is not so classified here because the private institutions in no way constitute a real private sector. They are scattered and diverse, and seldom are considered a category in general policy making. Among privately sponsored institutions are a few *grandes écoles*, Catholic universities, a couple of Protestant institutions, and some two dozen secular establishments; two-thirds of their students were also enrolled in public institutions until adjustments were made for them to transfer into the public institutions and so be eligible for the state degree.[1]

Iran might also be mentioned briefly because of possible confusion in its designation of types of institutions. Before the revolution, universities were divided between government and nongovernment institutions; however, the nongoverment institutions were "directly under the trust" of His Imperial Majesty or members of the royal family. They did enjoy less bureaucratic control and could advance at a faster pace. Their trustees had a freer hand and represented a broader spectrum of membership than the trustees of government institutions who were largely state officials.

The Iranian report comments on the former existence of private institutions but, since 1975, all post-secondary level education has been supported by the government. "Strictly speaking," the report says, "there are no private institutions of higher education still in existence in Iran." A few come under special status and are "more or less independent of government control—for example, the Iran Center for Management Studies and Damavand College."[2]

Neither Iran nor France has a functioning role for the private sector comparable to the other four countries. Thailand's private sector is small, enrolling only 6 percent of the students in higher education, but it is being encouraged to grow and play a more important part in the provision of places for students. Ten private colleges, oriented mainly to business training and related fields, have been established since the Private College Act of 1969 and, while they are supported from student fees that are generally sufficient to cover expenditures, they are nevertheless closely linked to government.

Although these institutions are not directly supervised by an official agency, the law provides for a Private College Commission having two representatives each from the government's Office of University Affairs and the National Education Commission, and three qualified persons appointed by the Cabinet. The Private College Commission recommends to the Minister of University Affairs regarding charters for such institutions, their programs, academic and financial operations, and the appointment of their directors upon nomination by the institution's trustees; the Commission also appoints an interim control board if a college runs into serious problems.[3] The ties are close regardless of private status and, in effect, all institutions in the different sectors of higher education in Thailand are responsible to one or several different government offices. Government universities are government departments.

For the first time in the planning process, in 1975, directors of private colleges were invited to confer with officials as the new National Education Development plan was designed. One matter agreed upon was "that private colleges should play a greater role through coordination and cooperation with the Office of University Affairs." And a significant policy statement was made calling for support to private colleges:

> ... to extend their programs in the fields they are ready for, so that they can fully share the tasks, and government higher education institutions will be able to devote their resources to other fields that private institutions cannot offer.[4]

Thailand is planning expansion for private institutions, anticipating their value in sharing tasks with the public sector, but it is also expected that the private arm will work more closely with the government ministry.

In Mexico, private institutions account for about 15 percent of the total number of students enrolled. Most private institutions must bear entirely their own costs. Public funds amount to less than 5 percent of their total budgets, and this amount goes chiefly to two institutions—El Colegio de México and the Instituto Tecnológico de Monterrey. Regardless of private status, authorization from a designated governmental body is required to validate their studies.[5]

The situation is very different in Japan. As part of the rapid expansion of higher education, the private sector has grown enormously and now accounts for 72 percent of the universities, 85 percent of junior colleges, and 11 percent of higher technical schools, which have been included in the higher education system since 1976.[6] Enrollment patterns accordingly show that 82.5 percent of college entrants in 1975 were in private institutions.

The increase in private institutions since the Second World War is very large, and the problems of the private sector are comparably great. With a ratio of nearly thirty one students to one faculty member (7.44 per teacher in national universities), classes are extremely crowded and quality and services for students drastically reduced. Income from student tuition cannot keep pace with expenditures, so the financial deficit is severe.

In 1974 the Ministry paid the differences between student fees and the costs for the national universities in the amount of $4,123 per student. The Ministry provided, however, only $177 ($167 toward operations and $10 for research) per student for private universities, which meant merely 4.2 percent of the aid needed to offset the deficit. By 1977—three years later— the government subsidy had risen to 26.9 percent of total operating expenditures for private universities, and the target established by the Private School Subsidy Law of 1975 was one-half of the operating expenses of private colleges and universities.

More important, the subsidy was based on evaluation of the performance of individual private institutions; it was a priority rationing along detailed lines calculated to improve the institutions.

> The ministry considers how well the university is fulfilling the national guidelines for higher education as well as the age of the institution, whether or not the university has internal problems, and whether the university's juridical body has failed to repay any debts to the Japan Private School Promotion Foundation, which provides state aid to the private school sector.[7]

One of the controls from the central government sets totals on enrollment for the private universities in order to lower the ratio of students to faculty and presumably improve standards for instruction and services. The "no-expansion" policy (except in specially needed fields) is accompanied by periodic financial reports to the central government, and allocations are biased toward institutions coming closest to the specifications. In short, the government is able to exercise control through subsidy policies and administrative guidelines, and the Japan Private School Promotion Foundation acts as its vehicle for funding. The Japanese report concludes:

> The Ministry of Education provides subsidies to private universities to help them out of their financial difficulties. As this assistance increased, the ministry became more and more involved with the problems of private institutions. Consequently, it is not inappropriate to question the degree of "privateness" and "publicness" of the private universities. There are two basic views on this issue: the first that private universities could probably receive up to a 50 percent subsidy from the government and still maintain their "privateness;" the second is that private institutions should only receive aid on a temporary basis and as soon as there is financial stability, the private institutions should refuse aid.[8]

The question raised by the Japanese concerning the degree of "privateness" is pertinent in the United States as public dollars flow in constantly greater amounts to private institutions, and the government, both federal and state, adds regulations and asks more accountability. Private higher institutions in the United States receive more than 35 percent of their total support from public sources.[9] The private sector is not independent financially. In 1979–80 federal student assistance alone reached approximately $7.8 billion including veterans' educational benefits.

In contrast to Japan, the United States private sector is strong and contains many of the highest quality institutions to which student competition for admission is greatest. The heritage of private higher education is long and honored, and it comprises more than half the total number of institutions of higher education in the country. Public institutions constitute 47 percent. Yet the public sector carries much more of the burden in enrollment with nearly 79 percent of the total number of students.[10]

Similar to Japan, however, private higher education in the United States also faces financial difficulty and seeks government subsidies. Tuition has gone up rapidly but seldom matches the spiraling costs and inflation. The problem will be compounded by the lower number of 18- to 21-year-olds just beginning to be felt in the typically college-age population. While private institutions have multiple sources of funds, such as income from endowment, philanthropic foundations, alumni, and charitable gifts given under tax exemption,[11] tuition remains the primary source.

Thus, the public dollar is eagerly sought after and recognized as a vital support for the private sector, thereby blurring the distinction in status between the public and private sectors. There is no question yet in the United States of controls from government that are as specific as those existing in Japan and Thailand, but other inroads have been made by government policies closely affecting private institutional operations as well as public. Evidence will be seen in later chapters about government actions concerning admissions, appointment practices, and graduate programs.

On tally, when higher education systems that have a private sector are compared with those that are generally public, the score does not necessarily add up to more erosion of autonomy in the public systems. Neither is there evidence that private sectors greatly influence government actions nor that they curb potentially excessive governmental regulations. Instead, their service is primarily toward expanding diversity and choice in curricular programs and opportunity for students. The are freer to innovate and to be more flexible in improving patterns of teaching and learning, but there is little proof that private institutions generally have taken such initiatives.

POWER OF THE PURSE

Even though Thailand, Mexico, Japan, and the United States have important sectors of private higher education, the governments are supporting, in various ways, more than half the total costs for all higher education. In the other eight countries, the governments pay the full price or close to it. In addition, most of them pay student subsistence allowances and charge little or no tuition. There cannot be much doubt as to who holds the heavier balance of power over the operations of higher education systems. The United States is, thus far, the exceptional case because of the relatively strong private sector, but the question raised is how strong the independent institutions will remain, considering present trends at both state and federal government levels and the general balance in funding sources.

In most of the countries, it would be thought ridiculous to suppose that any source other than government could financially support the higher education system. The French study specifically raised that question. Respondents were asked if they thought it "advisable to supplement state [central government] funding from other financial sources," which was explained to mean private funding, local or regional governments, or other state bodies. Answers reveal that no one imagines that any source other than the central government and associated public bodies could provide sufficient funds for essential needs.[12]

Perhaps the question was posed on the assumption that multiple funding sources could aid a system seeking increased autonomy for its units. Under the Orientation Law, the reform was outward—away from the strong and rigidly centralized tradition of the Paris government. The replies clearly show that people in higher education do not think it conceivable for the system to depart from established political authority and the well-worn, customary route to the central office.

Multiple funding sources can enhance freedom of operation and management of systems, but the principle is not guaranteed. It is a truism that the higher the percentage of total costs for higher education paid by central government, the greater are its directive and potentially dictatorial powers. On the other side of the coin, it is equally apparent that the more and varied sources for funding there are, the more potential authoritarian power is reduced.

Theorists talk about the advantages of having more than one governmental source of funds:

> Several levels of government are each responsible to the same voters, which may thereby keep them in check and balance.... A balanced division of responsiblity for the university campus keeps the citizens involved with university policy through at least two channels instead of one.[13]

Theoretically this is true, but one wonders how many citizens have knowledge about the higher education system, much less concern over one channel of responsibility compared to two channels. Public awareness is more apt to be focused on cost and whether higher education is even worth it at the end with so few jobs available.

The principle that division of responsibility and funding lessens the authority inherent in a single source is obviously valid. If the several funding sources are different levels of government, they can provide checks on each other or among themselves, which accordingly could restrain each one. The effective balance among them, however, is hard to find, much less to hold. Usually one partner is dominant and influences the decisive powers of the other.

There is the possibility and often the fact that instead of a check and balance function, one level may reinforce the other. The province or the local level may simply be the national government's tool in carrying out policies, acting in concert with and reinforcing the central position. Or, if the different levels of government are at odds over purpose and requests, the higher education system and single institutions are often torn to satisfy divergent and multiple demands. Collaborative manipulation and internal warfare are both possible, yet the principle remains that shared funding and powers are not as apt to decline into authoritarian rule as a single, central government retaining all funding power.

Again, the United States is unique in the significant amounts of private monies given to support higher education, particularly in the private sector. And, of late, such contributions are markedly increasing for public institutions as well. Leading state universities have launched big campaigns for funds among alumni and other sources besides the legislature. In addition, some have considerable endowment, like Berkeley from which one-third of its funds are drawn. This does encourage independence and even arrogance at times with regard to the state. But it must be remembered that this is unusual in the United States and unique among other nations.

NATIONAL–STATE LEVELS

Regardless of multiple funding, whether from levels of government or private sources, the main power lines potentially with the "payload" are those stretching to the national level of government. It is in this direction that higher education systems are generally moving, and at a fairly rapid pace. In unitary governments where the money and power are already located at the central level, the scene has not changed, but in certain instances the evidence of central power has become more apparent.

Sweden seems to have relaxed detailed regulations and maintained its informal customs, but the power center remains in the chancellor's office. While decentralization is being implemented in its reforms, significant changes have not yet been seen. France has attempted to promote independence and autonomy of universities, but the action continues to occur in the central office of the Minister of Universities (formerly Secretary of State for Universities). Poland proceeds with a high degree of centralization in control and funding, and so does Thailand.

Japan has increased the power and influence of the central minister's office and the national government pays an increasing share of total costs; and Iran shifted more power to the central level when the government picked up all costs for postsecondary education in 1975. In the United Kingdom, although federalism operates in relation to Scotland and Northern Ireland, the central government has greatly strengthened its hand in dealing with universities and the other sectors of higher education.

The federally organized countries and higher education systems present a slightly more complicated pattern in trends, but they are each gravitating toward government power, though it is not consistently on the national level. Australia has moved the farthest and most directly to national dominance, at least since 1974 when the federal Commonwealth took over full funding and abolished tuitions. Higher education policy is "now effectively made by one federal Minister of Education rather than by six state ministers."[14] With the advent of the new Tertiary Education Commission, unifying commissions for universities, colleges for advanced education, and technical and further education, the formerly separate sectors are joined in a national approach. Furthermore, the new commission is only advisory to the minister, who issues the guidelines within which their recommendations come.

Mexico, through the power of the purse, has largely nationalized higher education, regardless of the federal structure and state involvement. In 1976, the federal level was providing more than four-fifths of the total income for higher education. For the public sector alone, the federal government gave over 90 percent and the states contributed a little over 9 percent.[15] Evidence of the national concern over higher education has been expressed in many ways; most recently, it appeared in an expanded and reorganized central bureau including higher education.

Canada stands in opposition to the trend, but it would be a mistake to oversimplify the meaning of the last move on the part of the national government. Until 1966–67, universities in the provinces (except Quebec) received direct grants based on headcount. For the next ten years, the federal government provided funds by transferring tax revenues to the provinces—a scheme worked out earlier with Quebec. Then in 1977, arrangements changed again to make the federal influence even more indirect.[16]

No longer does the federal government share directly in costs with the provinces; instead, it is a combination of tax-point transfers and adjustment payments to increase and equalize provincial resources. The federal government posts its contributions for all to see; the provinces, however, allocate the resources. The post-secondary funds are linked with health funds which gives the province the decision between funding demands. Furthermore, the federal government discontinued its audit of higher education funds given to the provinces.[17] In short, Canada has entered a period of provincial dominance which holds, on the one hand, the dangers of provincialism in narrower and perhaps self-serving attitudes, but, on the other hand, offers a counterbalance to national power.

The present situation may be an uneasy balance in a transitional stage that could be reversed. Or, the forces at work in some of the provinces may foster the desire to return to the larger federal structure. For example, in a parliamentary debate on the university support vote in Ontario in 1978, demands were made for extreme interventionist planning and control by the provincial Minister of Education, including control of program offerings, the Canadian content of programs, faculty promotion policies, and relationships with other postsecondary institutions.[18] From the universities' point of view, such provincial controls would presumably be as reprehensible as similar controls from the federal government.

Reports from Quebec also reveal intense argument over stronger provincial control: the Quebec government named a commission of inquiry that suggested a new regulatory body to increase public control of institutions. The suggestion alone set off a heated debate, with universities, of course, saying that "government works best when it governs least." Another battle line was drawn when the government moved research from the inquiry and put it before a separate group preparing a "green paper" on all types of research in Quebec.[19] So, even though the operative power has been increased at provincial levels, the issue of further controls from government continues to plague the Canadian higher education system.

Circumstances are more ambivalent in the United States and the Federal Republic of Germany regarding the shared power between the federal government and the states or Länder. The pendulum has not swung definitively toward one or the other level of government; rather, both have exercised their powers more directly and in more areas affecting higher education systems.

Aside from specifically academic affairs which are discussed in a later chapter, the United States federal government has of late issued a whole host of regulations supporting some dozen pieces of legislation such as environmental protection, family rights and privacy, occupational safety and health, provision for the handicapped, and protection of human subjects in research. The laws and regulations fall under the role of government to protect the general welfare and pertain to all organizations, agencies, and business across the land, not just higher education. It is onerous nevertheless. More specific to higher education are conditions attached to the granting of funds to students and to institutions. Alan Pifer explains the latter rationale:

In general, it has been the fact of federal financial assistance to academic institutions that has given the federal government its right to interfere. Quite recently, however, at least one federal agency has been taking the position that the receipt of scholarship aid by students gives it the necessary standing to regulate the institutions attended by such students. This issue has yet to be fought out in the courts.[20]

To make matters worse, regulations have been pouring forth from various central agencies in an uncoordinated and inconsistent fashion which results in mountains of paper work for institutions at a high cost to the education programs. Lyman Glenny points out that "interventions into both procedural matters and substantive affairs have become sufficiently loathsome to warrant the creation" of a private commission by the Sloan Foundation to investigate the relationships of the federal government and higher education. But, he adds, intervention from the state level is even bolder.[21]

Historically, higher education systems are a state responsibility—in Germany as well as in the United States—and the states have therefore carried the larger share of funding. This is still true, but federal funds are growing, especially in student assistance programs. And federal controls and regulations continue to increase prodigiously, out of proportion to the growth in federal funds. The states are bearing a heavier share and tuitions are climbing. State relationships with public systems have always been close and often directive. Details of this connection are considered under planning and coordination; here the point is simply that state power, together with basic support, has greatly increased over higher education systems.

In West Germany, the situation is similar in the marked increase of both federal and Länder power, except that their rules and regulations are more excessive and extensive, and more confrontations have occurred. The passage of the Frame Law itself on the national level attests to the federal government's concern. Since 1970, federal policy has been toward greater expenditures on education and science, and accordingly, the Bund raised its portion of sales taxes to the Länder from 30 to 35 percent and gave additional funds to the financially weak Länder.[22]

Further, as part of higher education expansion, the Bund has invested in construction including student residences at a 50 percent subsidy to the Länder, and in financial aid to students at a 65 percent subsidy. Early in the 1970s tuition fees, which were only a small part of income, were abolished. So the federal share has increased considerably, though the Länder continue to bear the greater part of the financial burden.

Compared to the United States, however, West Germany has gone much farther in nationwide planning and centralized efforts such as in the placement of students. There is a Federal Minister of Education and Science, as well as several federal–state bodies of importance. (In 1979 the United States established a cabinet position for education, but it lacks size and extensive influence over higher education.) The growing strength at the national level has aroused antagonism in the Länder who have "autonomy" in operating higher education systems. And, as the drive toward centralization takes its course, frustration mounts as the Länder themselves cannot reach agreement, much less binding agreement, through the Conference of Ministers of Culture or the legislatures of the Länder.

So the Bund legislates and the Länder legislate further and implement according to their political inclination—which means some do and some don't. It is far from effective at the moment as a cooperative arrangement. The United States has not, as yet, entered this arena; it has no comprehensive educational plan for the whole country, no comparable "common tasks" between the federal and state levels, and the national Congress has shown less interest in higher education problems than the Bundestag.

In both the United States and the Federal Republic of Germany, the judicial branch of government has been more and more involved with higher education policies and procedures. For West Germany, the incidence of such cases is significantly greater, and its report states that in settling conflicts in the higher education sector, the Federal Constitutional Court has gained "an outstanding role in policymaking."[23] The report's authors consider this both good and bad. On the good side, "the legislative responsibility of parliaments is evoked" where adminstrative executive powers have prevailed in lieu of legal regulations. On the bad side, there is " the tendency to remit open issues of educational policy, disguised as law suits, to the courts . . . . Moreover, the increasing 'legalization' runs the risk of generating a narrow web of rules and regulations detrimental to any academic creativity."

The general thrust among the countries, regardless of whether the higher education system is unitary or federal in structure, is toward centralized power and the seat of finances. Such a direction is to be expected, especially in a time of tightening budgets which promote questions of value and accountability. Inside government and under legislative and, increasingly, judicial guidance, the locations of active power are in the executive branch, including the education ministry and the treasury or budget authority.

Within such a framework, which is typical for the majority of countries either on the state or national level, the higher education system is more than nominally a part of government; for all intents and purposes, it is an operational part. At this top level, the government draws at least the peripheral outline of the system, if not more details, by determining its total size—the number of student places, of faculty and assistants, of buildings, laboratories, and books in the library, and the amount of research monies. All are set by the total allotment of funds. In the same process and because they are necessarily concerned with student access, most governments decide on fees to be charged, if any, and subsistence allowances.

FINANCIAL ALLOCATION

As part of the grand design describing the outside limits of the higher education system, the procedures followed in financial allocation are crucial to the amount of administrative autonomy that may exist for one sector or another of the system and, of course, for individual institutions. John Millett has carefully summarized and compared the procedures used in the different structures: those where university budget requests go directly to the governmental budget office as in Iran and some states in the United States, and those in which requests are submitted by way of central ministries of education like Sweden, Australia, and the United Kingdom.[24]

After the "global" amount is decided upon in an appropriation bill, the distribution process becomes critical because the budget authority may allocate directly or the ministry may do so, with or without an intermediate body such as the University Grants Committee (UGC) in Britain which serves the university sector in this process. Most countries do not have such a "buffer" group comprised largely of academic representatives; instead, one government office or another will divide the funds and administer them with varying degrees of control. It is instructive to note that until recently the UGC dealt directly with the Treasury in this process, but now the buffer agency for universities is under the Department of Education and Science along with other sectors of the higher education system.

Formulas are employed by about half the countries in order to achieve some equity in treatment, but beyond this, the government also expresses its interest in expanding and extending learning opportunities in certain fields considered most needed by the society. Here is where the focus reveals the growing concern for vocational and career training, for continuing education for adults, and for specific fields like engineering and technical areas, graduate programs in Japan, and so on. "At some point in this process," Millett reminds us, "budget planning begins to assume all the characteristics of extensive program planning."

The total amounts awarded to higher education systems for many years increased steadily and occasionally dramatically, but, as Millett points out, the increases generally have slowed, universities feel disadvantaged, and tensions between universities and governments have heightened. Although most universities, as a favored sector in the educational systems, have had considerable internal budget authority, this too is changing with government concern for checking expenditures and stressing accountability.

Not many systems have government officers stationed actually within institutions to authorize all financial disbursements like the auditor–treasurer in each Iranian institution. He, in effect, is "operationally involved in the educational decision-making process,"[25] and he reports to the Ministry of Finance. Yet Thailand's Auditor-General's Office audits each institution whose funds are released by the Budget Bureau and the Ministry of Finance in line-item form. And in Thailand, universities prepare budget requests for each fiscal year in the same manner as any other government agency. Japan has executive administrators (distinct from presidents) directly appointed by the Ministry of Education to each public institution. They have charge of financial affairs and prepare the budget for the president, but they have no authority over personnel and curricular matters. In private institutions, executive administrators are appointed by the institution's board, although they work with the Ministry of Education on expenditure of government funds.

The Canadian report summarizes the situation for the other countries, who need only insert their own titles for the comparable offices. Edward Sheffield, commenting on the national scene, states that in spite of elaborate provisions for responsibility to such departments as the Ministry of State for Science and Technology and the Secretary of State:

> ...the real power remains in the Department of Finance, the Treasury Board, the Privy Council Office (of which the Federal-Provincial Relations Office is an important subdivision), and the Prime Minister's Office. These are the centers in which the crucial decisions are made, subject, of course, to the will of Parliament.[26]

The power of the governmental purse over higher education systems is very great indeed. It is definitive not just in total size of the system: it also has a profound effect on the several sectors of the system and their rate of growth or retraction. It further defines operations in many aspects of management and administration, and it has prompted the call for planning on a more comprehensive basis.

4
PLANNING

Governments may insist on planning for their higher education systems, but both they and the system appear to fail in the task. Societies generally have low marks in doing more than cope with today and the immediate future—even authoritarian societies that impose tight controls over their citizens and the economy. And as nations of the world become more interrelated in their economies, currencies, and the movements of people, planning ahead presents even more difficulties.

Higher education systems as social institutions are intricately tied to larger societal movements, although the fact is not always recognized by the academic mind. Predictions of student demand for entrance and choice of field for study, the availability of jobs for graduates, the attitudes of the population toward higher education, the amount of money to be allotted—basic ingredients for intelligent planning—depend heavily on the total society of which higher education is but one part. Hence, it is obviously hard to make assumptions and projections that will be fulfilled.

Planning in higher education is by its very nature based upon volatile units or "particles" that do not remain as defined, so results are often unpredictable. Some academics, therefore, consider it an exercise in futility, a waste of time and energy, but the counter argument is that without planning and some thoughtful, considered sense of direction, higher education systems are not apt to gain in political estimation or receive priority in the competition for finances. Blind faith in the goodness of higher education has been replaced by rational questioning.

Planning arises at each level where legal authority resides for allocation of resources. The need to conserve funds for priority functions and to meet new social demands requires planning of at least two years at the lower levels and up to five or ten years at higher levels. Ad hoc drifting does not very often result in the creation of higher quality programs of efficient use of resources. Planning makes those outcomes possible, if not fully guaranteed.

POLITICAL IMPETUS

Rather a recent phenomenon, the impetus for educational planning has largely come from political leadership. Only in Sweden and Poland has planning been operative since the Second World War. The other governments were later spurred into it by mass demands for education and the increasing costs for higher education. In all the countries of the study, however, with the exceptions of Mexico and Iran, the governments have taken the initiative either in requesting plans from the universities or ministries, or in making them through a series of major policy decisions that shape developments in their higher education systems.

At the same time, policy changes through political action are among the "volatile units" that can upset the best laid plans. For example, if the legislature or the executive branch suddenly decides to open access to higher education for a special and large segment of the population, i.e., adults or workers who need retraining courses, the plan may well have to be basically adjusted or altered, because the ground rules have changed. Similarly, compromises made between political parties and interest groups directly affect the neatest design for educational development. Over half of the countries in the ICED study draw attention, in one way or another, to the politics of planning and its effects.

Clearly, this discussion concerns systemwide planning on which each country's statements concentrated; less was said about institutional planning. Only occasionally does a report mention the institutional role and then it is particularly as a source of information and data. Government interest is primarily in comprehensive planning which takes into account relationships between or among the sectoral types of higher education in the total system.

BUDGETARY PLANNING

Since the political push for comprehensive planning and development is impelled especially by the financial limitations of the government, the first and foremost partner of educational planners is usually the treasury or budget bureau. In Sweden, where the Ministry of Education is more a planning than administrative agency, there is a planning and budget secretariat within it specifically to coordinate plans with the Ministry of Budget Affairs and the Ministry of Economic Affairs. Thailand and Poland both have national socioeconomic plans with higher educational planning as an integral part. Each of these countries operates on a five-year plan.

Higher education systems in the United Kingdom and Australia are on quinquennial and triennial budgetary plans, respectively, which, at least in the past, have constituted to a large degree their total planning. Projections are made, based on present assessment and evaluation, for both recurrent and capital funds. Regardless of the long-term projections, both national systems have been, in effect, on an annual budgetary basis due to financial exigency. Reports indicate they have partially returned to the rolling budgets. In Quebec, universities are on triennial budgets in principle, but annual budgets in operation, although capital costs continue on a five-year rolling plan. In practice, all Canadian provinces have annual budgets for universities.

In the other countries, higher education systems are also on annual budgets, which can scarcely be called even short-term planning. During the 1960s most states in the United States developed master plans for higher education. These plans were primarily incremental and quantitative, making additional student places available. However, in many states such plans also laid the basis for creating new community colleges, thus diversifying programs, opening access, and shifting the flow of students away from solely traditional college and university programs. Through such plans capital investments controlled the number of places available on each campus for each segment or sector in the system. The role and scope of each institution was thus defined.

Much recent planning has been less comprehensive and more closely tied to budgetary forecasting which, after all, is what the treasurer's office wants, but this has also been a limiting factor in educational thinking and projections. The question arises as to what the terms of reference are. What are the purposes of planning and how explicit are they?

TERMS OF REFERENCE

Planning for expansion of the higher education system is a pleasant undertaking. To this, the majority of the countries can bear testimony. Although planning was not a highly organized activity in the 1950s and 1960s, it produced new types of educational programs and many additional places for students. Today, among our countries, only the Federal Republic of Germany and prerevolutionary Iran speak of expansion; both have severe shortages in capacity for students.

Planning for contraction is the unhappy task now faced by those in most higher education systems. The problems are immense and complicated, many resulting from overexpansion, and exacerbated by diminishing funds. Beyond the issue of unused facilities which may be sold or converted to other purposes, the big problem is personnel, the number of faculty employed who have tenure or civil service status. Personnel costs constitute the main portion of total expenditures, and ways have to be found to retrain, reassign, or move faculty to other positions if the problem is to be solved. This, of course, is easier planned than done. Planning for decline requires more centralized decisions and strong leadership. As Clark Kerr has orally expressed it in discussion: "In expansion, the state legislature selected from what all institutions wanted to do; in contraction, the legislature selects from what none wants to do."

If the terms of reference for planning include student enrollment shifts in fields of study and manpower requirements, the complexity of the planning problems is great. As expected, more country reports named manpower needs as a focus for planning than any other area, but few know how to cope with the unknowns. The notorious undependability of manpower forecasts on which to base educational planning is well known, but even if projections were accurate, severe problems arise in the educational time lag for tooling up to offer the training needed and for graduating the students being trained.

Such problems are less acute in a country like Poland with a controlled economy operating within five-year planning frames. Under regulated conditions with detailed information on all personnel, manpower needs can be calculated with some accuracy, for example, in a field such as medicine. Jan Szczepański explains that the planners start with facts on age, training, and positions of present personnel; next they calculate losses due to death, retirement, migration, withdrawal for child bearing, and so on; then they consider birthrate and other demographic facts, and policy changes affecting geographic distribution, new institutions to be established, and new fields required for technological development and modernization of the economy. Subtracting the expected losses and adding the new factors yields the approximate number of places for students (even allowing for failures and dropouts), which fields of study, the length of time (since study courses are fixed in length), and the total costs involved. The report recognizes that this type of educational planning requires "a strong and efficient central administration."[1]

Sweden, on the other hand, which certainly has an enviable and sophisticated record in economic planning, does not claim effectiveness in manpower planning. Even though prediction of needs for graduates started in the 1930s, the U55 commission missed the mark widely in its estimates:

> Both needs and enrollments were grossly underestimated and had to be revised, only to be superseded once more, until suddenly the predicted shortages turned into surpluses, and increased enrollments turned into absolute decreases in the late 1960s.[2]

At issue is the response to admissions, which is basic to educational planning. Rune Premfors points out that in the manpower approach, admissions are matched to the predicted number of job openings in a particular field, while the social demand approach adjusts the number of places to the demand of applicants for that field. Sweden has followed both principles, tempered by the resources available, and so do most industrial countries.

Terms of reference for planning in higher education systems have long had a noticeably neglected area: the qualitative improvement of the system. While three country reports—Japan, Sweden, and West Germany—mention quality specifically as a concern, the approach to it is generally through quantitative controls or structural and physical reorganization.

Faculty development, methods of teaching, and reorganization of subject areas are seldom mentioned in educational planning. These elements are vital to the improvement of higher education systems and in some instances to cost effectiveness, but not many plans allow for retraining teachers, changes in pedagogical methods, or, for example, combinations of subject departments to promote multidisciplinary studies oriented toward society's problems. Societies have expressed their interest in and wish for such studies, in general terms, but the educational planners have not often included such substantive considerations in their terms of reference. Instead, the professors' inclination toward more limited specialization continues, reinforced by research, and this is accepted as a basis for planning.

The Japanese indicate their concern with quality improvement specifically in the private sector through their formula for support which is based on limits for enrollment. And their Ad Hoc Study Committee in its final report (after the 1973 energy crisis) shifted its plan from expansion to accommodate as many college aspirants as possible to a policy of slower growth and more selective expansion toward quality education. Thus, the political slogan was quality, not quantity.[3] Adjustments like this can encourage quality development, but the basic curricula and their educational content, as well as teaching abilities, are not directly approached.

According to the Swedish report,

> ...perhaps the most important organizational change from the point of view of planning was the creation of three bureaus of education and research.... Their significance was to derive from the fact that they integrated quantitative and qualitative planning.[4]

Formerly these two aspects were separated with the bureau of planning dealing with the quantitative aspects, and the bureau of education with goals, content, and structure of education. The newly combined bureaus are assigned not only the "what" of education, but also the "where" and "how much" in the planning process. Still, Premfors cautions that the division between these bureaus and the budget bureau is not clear, and, thus far, the latter seems to have the upper hand. However, Sweden has at least recognized the importance of qualitative aspects and has acted to place them immediately within the planning context.

West Germany's planning also calls attention to quality improvement. The goals set for the common tasks of the Bund and Länder in the Higher Education Construction Act include provision "...for a balanced relation between research and teaching, as well as a functional structure of higher education and innovation in modes of learning."[5] The authors of the report see these and other principles behind the building program as connected with far-reaching qualitative objectives, since they require policy decisions relating to number of places, and their distribution by region, field of study, and types of institution. Further, the decisions "...even affect aspects of study organization if, for instance, decisions are made as to the ratio between large lecture halls and smaller seminar rooms in the buildings to be constructed."[6] Physical space does influence methods of teaching, but then "lectures" are frequently delivered by the professor, so conditioned, in the "seminar" room.

Planning in the Federal Republic of Germany is based on a "space-related" study place, which is given a standard value that is multiplied by the number of places needed to give the amount of construction required, which is then converted to cost. It is basically quantitative and structured primarily on present concepts of instruction. Goals offer imaginative possibilities, but human limitations enter into the concrete building plans.

An issue related to quality considerations and typically omitted in planning processes is the use of educational research, which very few countries take seriously into account. The Swedish system again is the exception in its close relationship between educational planners and educational research in higher education, although the West German report points toward considerable advance in this direction. In specific areas, and from what is still a relatively small number of institutes for these purposes, educational research is becoming significant in regional planning and in considering connections between the educational and employment systems.[7]

The conclusion is that planning in higher education systems in most countries around the world remains primarily quantitative, financial, and physical. These considerations far overshadow qualitative aspects which, admittedly, are even harder to plan for than the quantitative.

METHODS AND PROCESS

Although the terms of reference and purposes for planning may be clearly delineated, the process is difficult to execute, both in assembling the facts needed and in projecting very far into the future in view of the unknown elements that can abruptly alter plans. Too often planning breaks down at the beginning of the process, regardless of an elaborate superstructure created by agencies, committees, and institutions. In the first place, the facts are missing, inaccurate, or controversial. Whether human error or computer programming is to blame, the basic ingredients can be undependable. It becomes more complicated when comparative statistics are required to permit analysis among institutions and allow compilation for a particular sector or for the whole system.

Statistical collection and data gathering are relatively new fields, just as planning itself is a rather recent art and, as frequently observed, not a science. Repeatedly, the country reports complain that specialized personnel are not available to do the job (Iran and Mexico), that data collection is ad hoc and unsystematic (Thailand), and even nations more advanced in the planning art like Sweden, the United States and West Germany record their troubles.

The Bundestag passed the Law of Statistical Data for Higher Education in 1971 "in order to improve the notoriously deficient educational statistical data." Besides trying to achieve uniformity and accelerate the process, data collection was to include information on study programs, length of study and successful completion, and personnel, as well as on space and other financial aspects. Problems, nevertheless, have persisted and have handicapped the planning process.[8]

Another problem area in methods and process is the time frame projected in the planning. If we are correct in calling the basic elements volatile particles, then the resultant plan cannot be expected to remain applicable for long in its present form. Only the short-term can hold fairly stable due to assumptions on which it is based, and even that is subject to outside catastrophic events in society. Such difficulties are recognized in the countries on three- or five-year budgetary planning. Actually operations proceed on an annual basis, and "rolling" or "cyclical" mechanisms are employed for review and adjustment thereafter. As the time span ahead increases, projections are bound to decrease in accuracy and therefore applicability to a changed set of circumstances.

Japan's Ad Hoc Committee, working with the Ministry of Education, has divided its ten-year projection to 1986 into two five-year stages with the first quite "strict and exact" while the second remains open for further consideration.[9] For adjustments to changes in objectives and financial planning, the Federal–State Commission in West Germany is preparing educational budgets on a model that has a "what if" character. Given variations of input, the model permits calculations of personnel, space, and costs for higher education as well as the entire educational system. This was the way adjustments were made in the first intermediate-term plan when earlier projections were not fulfilled.[10] Alternative or contingent planning, in one way or another, is obviously essential to meet the chance element in assumptions and predictions.

West Germany is by far the most ambitious and courageous of the countries in extending the Comprehensive Educational Plan produced for 1973–85 to the year 1990. This is "an expansive, quantitative development program" with "general basic decisions about the structure of the educational system that is to be attained." It is this plan, agreed upon by the Bund and the Länder, which introduced long-term planning of goals and cost calculation. Before this, intermediate four-year financial planning had been practiced.[11]

The United States, Canada, the United Kingdom, and Australia have no comprehensive plans like those in Japan and West Germany or, for that matter, in Sweden, Poland, or Thailand. In Australia, the stage is set with the new Tertiary Education Commission, but as yet there is no indication of such planning.

Most individual states in the United States had established planning mechanisms by 1968, but with widely varying powers and organization. Multicampus systems and other types of programs in the public sector developed through planning guidelines under state auspices. Not until the 1970s, however, were many plans extended to incorporate all public sectors and private institutions. This extension is explained in the next chapter on coordination. The United States is way ahead in planning functions, but it is a state achievement and not national in scope.

Farther away from total planning are Iran and Mexico, confronted with the lack of basic data, although the National Association of Universities and Institutions of Higher Education in Mexico is working on this problem. Its member institutions have been urged to establish offices for collecting information; some data has been pulled together on the national level, and agreement reached on terminology to be employed.[12]

Reviewing the status of planning reveals an exceedingly wide range of use and varying degrees of effectiveness. Throughout, the crucial issue is whether the higher education system is planning for qualitative improvement (few are) or whether planning merely copes with current demands by ad hoc changes to avoid trouble in the system. In too many countries, the latter approach is prevalent: planning is in response to crisis and is quantitative in approach. There is little indication that long-range thinking and imaginative ideas have entered the planning forum. Too many countries still reflect the educational programs and the general thinking of the bygone era of the 1960s.

5
COORDINATION

With the complexities and expansion of higher education systems have come increased efforts to coordinate the various parts. As different sectors of educational institutions have emerged and grown—some spectacularly—in the various countries, their relationships to each other have been tenuous or nonexistent. Coordination is, therefore, a most important purpose of planning: it is at the heart of management and administration within one institution, and a central function of the upper levels of sectors and the whole system of higher education.

Thirty years ago, coordinated activity among institutions of higher learning was seldom mentioned, and the word *systems* certainly did not apply in this context. As long as higher education was for a relatively few people and institutions held their individuality, there was little thought about interrelated activity and planning. But mass education changed that, just as it changed the nature of the educative process, the fields for teaching, and most other aspects of higher education. Not only has the concept of systems appeared, but coordination has become the answer to many pervasive problems in higher education.

Coordination, in the country reports, has been dealt with primarily as an aspect of control or part of the power structure in systems. Burton Clark takes this position in his searching analysis of "Coordination: Patterns and Processes."[1] He shows the structure of embedded power from the professor to the national level and several patterns that have emerged. He describes the interplay of forces, formal and informal, in various processes of coordination.

The discussion that follows singles out a few of the main purposes for coordination. What are the aims of coordination? What are the problems of systems today that especially require coordinated activity? Why coordinate? After suggesting a few of the main purposes, the discussion concentrates on the principal methods being tried by different countries. Again, attention is directed, unless otherwise noted, at systems, not single institutions, although the institutions themselves are integral to both the problems and the methods.

AIMS

Too often coordination is either treated as an end in itself or is considered the only solution to a vague and extensive array of problems. Interpretation of the word as an aspect of power tends to broaden its application and include some activities that are better left to uncoordinated development and creative, individual initiative. This differentiation has not been made sufficiently. Thus, in selecting only three aims for coordination, the intent is to recognize the main problem areas where coordinated efforts are especially pertinent and needed.

Efficiency

Probably the most frequently mentioned aim for coordination is to avoid waste, eliminate duplication, and improve operations. The need for such improvement, of course, hits single institutions as well as systems. Concepts of efficiency—flow charts and techniques of systems management—have been transferred from business enterprise to the academic setting.

Higher education systems are found to be exceedingly wasteful of their resources, an unpardonable sin in the market place where time and money are carefully tended. Business-oriented minds, ignorant of higher education's peculiar practices in handling its affairs, express concern that faculty personnel are not in classrooms eight hours daily, that physical plant is not fully utilized, that class scheduling lacks a clear rationale, and that purchasing is not always put out for competitive bids. These seem odd, if not unreasonable, practices. Cost effectiveness has been inadequately applied.

Although it is true that the nature of the educational process is difficult to measure and the "product" eludes easy definition in business terms, there is considerable justification for criticism and for the demand that results be evaluated. Accountability has risen as a major issue in many countries, especially as higher education systems compete with other areas of expenditure for financial resources.

To improve efficiency, policies and practices have to be related to each other—coordinated for smooth and effective operations. In higher education systems, the links between policy and practice have been loose and sometimes lacking altogether. Under these circumstances, details of management and administration have assumed importance, and regulatory rules have proliferated. The lines of control have tightened as hierarchy has grown into systems and enlarged central offices for the execution of policies.

Earlier we considered government's power and influence in funding. The government's role now is seen as an invasion into administrative and management affairs, which is pronounced and evident. The West German report makes it clear:

> ...that the resulting loss of autonomy concerns partly areas in which the universities themselves had been ineffective and which, for reasons of efficiency, the government now considers it necessary to take over.[2]

In the name of efficiency, extensive changes are being made in governing and administering higher education systems, and coordination is a favored approach to solve the problems.

Equitable Distribution

A second problem to be resolved through coordination is the need for more equitable distribution of higher educational opportunities which have tended toward concentration in urban areas. Regional neglect is recognized by many countries. France, for example, has adjusted its formula for financing to aid provincial institutions and enhance their power to attract enrollment away from Paris and its vicinity. Thailand has eased entrance requirements of some institutions in outlying areas to encourage students; Japan had as its goal to set up universities in each prefecture, and has done so.

Canada and Australia have large rural areas whose people do not have access to higher education in any way comparable to those in the more populated regions. Western Canada has started community colleges and extension services; Australia, in addition to new institutions, has encouraged the growth of technical and further education programs throughout the country. Well over half of the programs are outside the six capital cities.[3] Although the United States has built some outstanding state universities, and private institutions are scattered across the country, two-year community colleges located nearer students' homes are the predominant means for reaching outside the large urban areas.

Even the smaller countries like the United Kingdom, Poland, and the Federal Republic of Germany have expressed concern with problems of geographic dispersal in their higher educational systems. Several countries have used communication media and extension courses, and many have established new institutions in areas with insufficient opportunities. Now the fledgling institutions remain to be nurtured, frequently at a cost to the older institutions, and to be integrated into the system.

In opposition to areas lacking access to higher institutions, and especially lacking selection in types of study programs, are geographic areas inundated with institutions where duplication exists among courses offered. Thus, courses are under-enrolled, faculty inefficiently employed, and physical facilities inadequately used. The problems of efficiency arise again in this context.

Particularly in specialized fields like engineering, veterinary medicine, Russian, East Asian studies, and other costly subjects, institutions need to be selected carefully with regard to location as well as expertise in qualifications. To do this requires coordinated planning and control. During the expansionary era, sights were not focused on such possible consequences: growth was all-absorbing. Planning frequently fell short and, as a result, higher education systems were not balanced either in their offerings or in the location of institutions. Coordination is necessary.

Diversity

The improvement of efficiency and equitable distribution of programs were specifically mentioned in the country reports as purposes for coordination. The third aim is selected because of its conspicuous absence: country reports seldom mention the preservation of diversity as a goal for coordinated activity. The authors may assume the enduring existence of differences among the system's sectors, but to take it for granted is a risky position in the face of current trends. Strengthening and sharpening diversity should be explicitly stated as a primary purpose for coordination.

There is a powerful undertow in the educational order of society known as "academic drift" that seems to be a natural force afflicting systems everywhere. It comes, in part, from less prestigious institutions of higher education emulating those occupying positions of respect and favored treatment. Britain has seen polytechnic institutions inching toward universities; in the United States, teacher-training institutions have moved toward liberal arts colleges which, in turn, have added masters-level programs imitating universities.

Australia presents a pertinent example of the erosion of diversity and where it leads. The colleges of advanced education were formed partially from older technical and teachers' colleges and, as first defined, they were to offer courses for the diploma level, not degrees. Within little more than ten years after degree-granting status was later given the colleges, 30 percent of students were in first degree courses and 7 percent in postgraduate courses. Although some undoubtedly consider this beneficial in siphoning off heavy enrollments from the universities, Bruce Williams notes that it has led to overlap and duplication which have provided "evidence that there were economies to be achieved through 'rationalization.' "[4] (The term refers to coordination with a rationale developed for improved relationships and planning among the sectors.)

Meanwhile, in the technical and advanced education sector of Australia, students were registering less in technical courses and more in vocational courses, especially paraprofessional fields, which also involved growing competition with the colleges of advanced education. Here the overlap in courses has resulted in searching questions about the relative standards of the certificate and diploma courses offered by the two sectors.[5]

The multipurpose sector in the middle—colleges for advanced education—experiences the problems of overlap with the domains belonging to the sectors on each side, the university sector on the one hand, and the technical and advanced further education sector on the other. The broader the purposes of institutions, the more overlap will inevitably occur with educational programs in other sectors. Lines cannot be held inviolate between sectors if multiple programs are to be available at comprehensive or multipurpose institutions, but conscious decisions should be made to allow for overlap when desirable. At least it need not be the result of mere imitation, chance, or haphazard planning.

Academic drift results not only from the impulse to imitate the university; it also comes from the creation of more comprehensive institutions and from the practice of trying to upgrade quality by lifting the status of institutions. Each of these forces encourages the trend toward overlap and increasing similarity among institutions and thereby reduces diversity.

Furthermore, coordination itself possesses compelling forces for integration which can lead toward conformity and standardization. The urge to pull the disparate pieces into a pattern for harmonious action seems almost instinctive, if not irresistible. Caryl Haskins, in his excellent analysis *Of Societies and Men*, compares the evolutionary process in nature with the development of integrated, well-coordinated social communities as a mechanism for survival. But, then he observes that "increasing integration through tighter and tighter organization and greater and greater subordination of the parts to the whole" eventually reduces the parts to helpless dependents. Society reaches ultimately a totalitarian state.[6]

Fear of such an outcome is expressed by some educational spokesmen seeing all too much uniformity resulting from indiscriminate adherence to policies and operational guidelines intended to achieve efficiency, eliminate overlap, and aid coordination. Haskins goes on to describe resistant trends that can move back toward "greater overall simplicity and sharper specialization."[7] These counterforces should be specified as directions for aims of coordination. The aims should be to improve efficiency through greater simplification and to protect diversity by sharpening specialization and differences in courses given by the various sectors of higher eduction systems.

Thus far, it has proven harder to maintain diversity effectively with pride in the distinctive purposes of institutions than to ease into amalgamation with tidy, coherent patterns. Yet the preservation of diversity in programs is the only way to serve the needs of the growing clientele who are of different ages, and come to higher education from different walks of life and for different reasons.

Too many countries' systems seek coordination—almost as an unquestioned end in itself—with little foresight or imagination concerning what is being coordinated and where the effort may lead. The process of coordination certainly exists throughout the power structure of systems; and under its aegis, the controls have shifted position and extended their direct influence. But this is only part of the truth. The main point is the end in view—the reasons for coordination. It is imperative that purposes be thoughtfully considered and explicitly stated. Then the most promising method can be selected.

METHODS

Efforts to coordinate systems have produced a medley of methods, and sometimes the efforts themselves need to be coordinated. Often the approach is too simplistic, reflecting ignorance of the complexities involved and the characteristics of the higher education enterprise in which many elements are acting and interacting without predictability. Some schemes for coordination seem to have been invented by an overly theoretical mind isolated from the realities of the situation. Other schemes are so vague and open ended that the initial confusion is merely compounded.

By far the largest number of significant difficulties have come from the former approach—the logic applied to charts of command stations. In many instances, organizational logic has outdistanced function and ushered in often meaningless growth in the superstructure for controls. New bodies have been formed and additional responsibilities given to existing offices which means more personnel and agencies. The consequence is lengthening the vertical hierarchy and broadening the horizontal lines not just on the governing chart, but in actual operations. This multiplies bureaucracy and costs, increases rules and regulations, and frequently creates waste and inefficiency—the very diseases coordination is intended to cure.

Bureaucracy and Regulations

Higher education systems are microcosms of the larger webs of bureaucracies in government. In 1976, the United States is reputed to have had 90 separate regulatory agencies in Washington issuing 7,000 new rules every year. Estimates of the cost of government regulation reach as high as 100 billion dollars annually. President Carter initiated plans to revise the regulatory process by creating a review board and a council to coordinate efforts of the various agencies. It is, in effect, another agency to coordinate, but it recognizes that Americans' contact with their government is "a bewildering mass of paperwork, bureaucracy, and delay."[8]

The President's intent is to cut government costs, but what about the costs of compliance borne by those affected? Higher education systems are not spared this troublesome task, costing heavily in time and money. It is estimated that the University of California system alone spends about 5 million dollars a year in replying to requests from state and federal governments and national organizations. The amount is multiplied many times for the systems in each of 50 states.

West Germany's situation is similar to the United States in plethora of paperwork, and their report also emphasizes the proliferation of committees and meetings and demands upon professors' time in attempts at coordination in their federalist system of higher education. Sweden selects bureaucratization as one of the major trends and defines it simply: "the increase in the number of bureaucrats—the increase in their influence on higher education as well as the increase in the complexity of the formal rules of the system."[9]

Sweden, however, starts from a smaller base to build bureaucracy. The 14 ministries altogether have less than 2,000 employees, though ad hoc commissions (about 300) with considerable staff are tied to the ministries. The reason for the small number in the Ministry of Education, for example, is that its functions are limited to policy planning and preparation of laws and budgets. More routine planning and administration are performed by central agencies of which there are about 70 for all ministries.[10] Nevertheless, bureaucracy is on the rise in Sweden.

It should be added that Canada and Australia, as well as the United Kingdom, reflect a slower growth in bureaucracy than the other countries mentioned. Custom and tradition may be factors in their resistance to Parkinson's principle, and the comparatively less affluence of these nations may further help curb the growth. Whatever the reasons, their reports in the study do not reflect the problems of dealing with burgeoning bureaucracy to the same degree as the others. Still, they do indicate similarity in expanding regulations and controls.

As long as governments legislate coordination for systems, the tangle of regulations is likely to grow. The legislative method has not proven highly effective and secondary complications can be severe, but laws are the machinery at hand. When he expressed concern over regulations, President Carter acknowledged as much: "For too long, we have acted as if we could throw another law or another rule at every problem in our society without thinking seriously about the consequences."[11]

Within the framework of laws stating policies and sometimes procedures, higher education systems in the different countries function with
numerous variations in patterns. But from the great variety of methods, two
types of organizations emerge: central authorities and intermediate bodies of
one sort or another.

One would expect countries with unitary political organization to assign
primary responsibility for coordination to national, central ministries, and
federally organized countries to allot the task to provincial or state offices
where responsibility rests for higher education systems. The expectation,
however, turns out to be only partially fulfilled. Both unitary and federal
nations are using intermediate bodies and, contrary to the assumption, some
federal governments have taken the initiative, especially in coordinative
planning and operations, regardless of the legally assigned duty to the states.
Australia and the Federal Republic of Germany are examples. Therefore, to
simplify the complexities, this summary deals with centralized authority
(whether on national or provincial levels) and intermediate agencies which
include regional bodies.

Central Authorities

Burton Clark claims that "central bureaucracy cannot effectively coordinate mass higher education." This is the first lesson he would have
Americans learn from the experience of others abroad. It is most relevant
since the United States has recently established a national Department of
Education with cabinet status. Clark's reasoning goes along these lines. In
view of the great mixture of many students and ever widening fields of study
with mass higher education, the increased complexity of tasks demands:

> (a) plural rather than singular reactions, or the capacity to face simul-
> taneously in different directions with contradictory reactions to contra-
> dictory demands; (b) quicker reactions, at least by some parts of the system,
> to certain demands; and (c) a command structure that allows for myriad
> adaptations to special contexts and local conditions.[12]

And Clark concludes that "a unified system coordinated by a state bureaucracy is not set up to work in these ways." It resists differentiated and flexible
approaches.

Aside from the likelihood of rigidity and the absence of flexibility in
most government offices on any level, in any area of supervision, there is the
question of whether coordination is really achieved, even if it is detrimental.
The evidence is thus far rather negative in the 12 countries of our study. With
the exception of Poland, which may be presumed to have its command
structure under clear directives laid down by the larger economic and social

plans, the countries having central ministries to coordinate their systems do not show remarkable achievement.

Thailand presents a most elaborate and intricate organization chart with lines from higher educational institutions leading into at least five different ministries, though the majority are under the Office of University Affairs and the Ministry of Education. All institutions are part of government, and the Council of Ministers reigns at the top. But then, there are three subsystems or sectors of universities, private colleges, and government colleges, each with its coordinating group or groups. Membership on the various commissions and coordinating groups is customarily designated by virtue of the position held or by appointment of the cabinet. It is a highly formalized structure. Assessing its effectiveness, the report concludes:

> ...that a certain degree of coordination and control, whether desirable or not, has been achieved in each subsystem of higher education. But coordination or collaboration over the whole spectrum of higher education in Thailand is yet to be seen.[13]

With all the structure, lines and charts, and all the regulatory controls from central offices, coordination in large part escapes the bureaucrats.

France, until the reform of 1968, was the archetypal pattern of a central authority in which responsibility resided for coordination as for most other needs of the higher education system. Yet, no one ever claimed coordination of the system's parts. One has only to glance at the preferential status given the *grandes écoles* as a separate and special category. Moreover, all higher education was not, and is not today, unified under the Ministry of Universities; other ministries supervise different institutions. So a central pattern does not necessarily mean unified action even when the cabinet level, as in Thailand, becomes the final coordinator. The coordinative process gets lost in the ministers' separate domains.

Sweden has solved that problem fairly well; the centralized authority for the system has gradually been consolidated. In 1976, the new National Board of Universities and Colleges supplanted some five central agencies and boards, leaving only the University of Agricultural Sciences and teacher training outside the national board's scope of operational authority. A functional order of unity exists at the central agency level, and the instruments for coordination are structurally there. But at the moment of accomplishing nearly complete centralization, Sweden decided to decentralize the system in part by establishing regional boards. These will be discussed in the next section on intermediate bodies.

Japan, too, has a high degree of structural unity in the national Ministry of Education which has existed for a long time—since nationalistic policies were introduced at the beginning of modernization by the Meiji government.

In the last decade, the ministry has reasserted its role in coordination and especially planning. While much attention has gone toward long-term planning for enrollment and facilities, the guidelines issued in 1972 are most perceptive in recognizing the elusive combination of "respecting the spontaneity [and creativity] of institutions" at the same time government financial assistance is given and stipulations are made for reform.[14]

The guidelines call for a national coordinated plan that aims at the full utilization of resources by different types of institutions, training in necssary specialized fields, and ensuring a fair regional distribution of institutions. Japan has stated its purposes for coordination; the means of achieving them rest in the central bureaucracy. An official, national plan for coordination of the system has not appeared in the eight years following the guidelines.

Central agencies in unitary nations are clearly the loci of power and responsibility but, adequate as the command structure may be, it has thus far proved unable to achieve effective coordination, particularly of the various sectors of higher education in a total system. As a result, most nations say that several systems actually exist and the concept of a single comprehensive system remains theoretical.

When the central authority rests operationally at the provincial or state level, which has usually been the case in federally organized countries, the results are not greatly different. Only here the picture is clouded somewhat by relative shifts in the positions of the dominant elements. First there is the influence exerted by the national level as the growing source of subsistence. Australia and the Federal Republic of Germany have moved most noticeably in this direction. Second, there is the situation, as in the United States and Canada, where the states or provinces reflect in detail the same problems as those existing at national levels in unitary nations. And, from the institutional vantage point, similar demands issue forth from state departments of education and boards of control of one type on another.

In the first instance of Australia and the Federal Republic of Germany, both national governments have expressed increasing concern about coordination in higher education and have acted in accordance with perceived needs as their financial contributions have grown. States have, in part, given way and now share the role which formerly belonged to them alone as a primary responsibility. In Germany, the federal government has taken leadership in the Frame Law of 1976, especially for concerted planning on a highly detailed and specific basis; in Australia, the Commonwealth Government has brought the three main sectors of higher education together in the new national commission established in 1977.

In both countries, state level authorities are active participants and constitute structurally another "central" agency with which institutions must deal. Although the Australian states no longer contribute financially (except in the technical sector), they continue their operational functions and serve as the channel for federal funds to institutions. Each state has a statutory authority to coordinate colleges for advanced education, but only two have any such mechanism for universities; and the technical and further education sector is under supervision of one or more state departments. Thus, although the funding is unified nationally and the federal commission is responsible for all three sectors, the state level is not so coordinated. Various organizational bodies and departments are involved, universities remain largely outside state coordinative efforts, and there is no evidence of effective coordination on a general scale.

Germany's Länder retain more power with their significant share in the funding, and they have been assigned the task of carrying out the coordinated planning mandated by the Frame Law. The concept of common tasks between the Bund and Länder has emphasized partnership and cooperation toward "cultural federalism" especially to bring about uniform living conditions, including educational components, throughout the republic. Most of the activities, however, have been planning for facilities and construction. The West German report makes clear that the mixed system of Bund and Länder represents "a compromise which is not altogether adequate."[15] It sounds like détente between two power levels, one of which—the Länder—cannot reach consensus in coordinating their position or their programs in higher education.

In contrast, the other federally organized countries in this study—the United States, Canada, and Mexico—have no comparable national power centers. Instead, the responsibility for coordination still rests basically with the states or provinces in the first two countries, while it largely remains a matter for voluntary associations in Mexico. And the prognosis for effective leadership in Mexican voluntary associations is not very encouraging. It is suggested that the National Council of Science and Technology (CONACYT) and the more recently created office for Coordination of Higher Education, Science, and Technology could provide some coordination, particularly in research, but "they probably will either be semi-independent and ineffective or increasingly government-controlled and possibly effective. Mexico has nothing approaching the power of the stronger United States statewide planning boards."[16]

Compared to Mexico, of course, Canada and the United States have highly organized state powers that, in higher education systems, are determinant influences, and coordination is definitely within their territories. It is here one finds the equivalent of central authorities in the unitary nations. Among the ten provinces of Canada, the patterns of organization and attempts at planning and coordination are perhaps as varied as those in the 50 United States, where patterns tend to be repeated and resolve themselves into four or five general, predominant types.

Canada's range of patterns is wide and the differences are great in the various developmental stages of provincial structure for higher education. From the ten variations, Edward Sheffield singles out Quebec and Alberta as closest to having system-wide planning toward "complementarity" to reduce needless duplication and identify the strengths and directions at least for universities.[17] The two provinces goals are the same, but their processes differ. Quebec's planning structure involves individual universities, the intermediary Council of Universities, the Conference of Rectors and Principals (a voluntary association), and the higher education division of the Ministry of Education. Alberta, on the other hand, has a simplified process with fewer bodies involved: principally the universities and the Department of Advanced Education and Manpower.

Ontario, too, has sought coordination of its higher education system. In fact, since 1951, when a broad order was issued by the provincial council to establish a close liaison between the government and the universities for greater coordination of the universities' work and advice to the government on financing policies, a series of committees has come and gone.[18] Today, informality has been replaced by a rather formal pattern in which the Council of Ontario Universities (represented by their presidents) and the Ontario Council on University Affairs (advisory) deal with the government's Ministry of Colleges and Universities, which has steadily increased its central authority.

The colleges of applied arts and technology have a governing Council of Regents, and the sector is answerable to the Ontario central ministry. The smaller sectors of agricultural technology and health-related professions are connected with other appropriate ministries; and so again, we find the lack of system-wide coordination at the provincial ministerial level. Not unlike France and Sweden, the overall structure is present, at least in the composition of the top governing body, but comprehensive coordination of the higher education system has not occurred.

At the other end of Canada's spectrum of patterns are the Maritime provinces which have joined together in a higher education commission under the leadership of their premiers, but recommendations return to provincial legislatures and premiers for final decisions. New institutions have arisen without the commission's blessing even though one of its several mandated tasks is to advise on new courses and needs.[19] At best, the organization is loose and lacks power to coordinate the post-secondary institutions.

In comparison to Canada's disparate pattern, the United States presents a somewhat more consistent design of general types of planning and coordinating bodies for the states' higher education systems, but the categories shield myriads of smaller variations among the states. Nevertheless, the majority have coordinating agencies or consolidated boards that serve this purpose in addition to other assigned functions. Most are regulatory over the institutions in their system, but some are advisory and therefore influential in direct proportion to the effectiveness of their leadership and the attention given them by political offices.

In 1972, coordination received a strong boost from the federal government in the Amendments to the Higher Education Act of 1965, which called for the establishment of "1202 Commissions" (so called from the section number amending Artical XII).[20] States were required to designate an existing body or establish a new one for comprehensive, statewide planning for post-secondary education, which was defined very broadly to include all public and private institutions, proprietary, technical and vocational schools and institutes, and community and junior colleges. The designation of a 1202 Commission was necessary for the state to receive federal funds, particularly for community colleges and occupational education—most vital programs and the fastest growing. Furthermore, the federal government paid the expenses of the commissions for "proper and efficient administration," and offered technical assistance with the necessary appropriation. Forty six states have named such commissions; only four have not and so are not eligible for the federal funds stipulated in the amendment.

Coordinating functions had long been assigned to state boards and agencies, so 31 states simply named existing bodies to comply with the federal action, but frequently the boards were increased in membership to broaden representation. Well over half the states, in this way, combined the newly expressed federal concern for coordinative planning and programs with their former structure for higher education systems. Regardless of the type of agency that has evolved, there are no brilliant examples of statewide coordination of the higher education institutions.

It is quite important to observe, however, that although some states have been pushing for cooperative controls for as long as two decades, the drive has been strengthened of late and, accordingly, centralized authorities—in state capitols—are more directive, and "super-boards" are more regulatory.

Progress has certainly been made toward coordination of higher education systems in the states, but the price may prove to have been high when viewed from a future perspective. Centralized authorities inherently choose regulations as the method and, for regulations to hold, they must be fairly specific and well-defined. This is where rigidity is apt to set in, thus distorting the intended purpose and stifling creative, imaginative solutions. Moreover, central bodies, especially those of a political nature, harbor the dangers of decision making on issues vital to higher education by persons distant from the campuses, often unfamiliar with the problems and hence the possible effects of their decisions.[21]

Yet, centralization is the easiest route to follow, organizational charts lead naturally to controls at the top, and governments want to see *comprehensive* pictures of how the public funds are spent and who is being served. So the movement in this direction continues, even though central authorities have not shown remarkable success in efforts to coordinate the several sectors within their systems, and they pose hazards to the healthy functioning of higher education.

Intermediate Bodies and Decentralization

While central authority gains, many intermediate bodies operate providing in some ways, a counterforce, to centrality, and assisting the general functioning of the higher education system. A strong case can be made for the effectiveness and importance of the intermediate agency in developing cooperative attitudes and programs that may well further genuine coordination more than centralized actions.

Intermediate bodies are defined by a combination of characteristics which stem from certain alternatives. They are either:

1. statutory or voluntary organization;
2. regional or national in scope;
3. general or specialized in interests.

The first two alternatives are clear, but the third may require a bit of explanation. If the group represents, say, only universities or technical institutes, it would obviously reflect the special interests of its constituency. But, if the group is comprised of the Ministers of Education from the ten provinces as in the case of the Council in Canada, or the Conference of Ministers of Culture and Education from the eleven Länder in West Germany, it naturally reflects the general interests of education, not the specific concerns of one sector.

Depending on the combination of characteristics, the intermediate agency's organization, scope and interests are set and, to a partial extent, its power may be circumscribed. Certainly that is true if powers are outlined by statute. Further, if the agency is a national body speaking for a special interest, it is more likely to have a sharper focus and represent a larger number of constituents, which will make it a political force not to be ignored. One has only to look at a strong lobby at work in parliamentary halls to see the potential. The analogy may be distasteful in the decorum of educational circles, but it is none the less apt, except that higher education groups are seldom as well organized as, for example, the oil interests in advancing their cause.

Another, perhaps more acceptable, analysis of the role of intermediate agencies suggests that their influence and power are tied to their position in the structural hierarchy of the higher education system; the importance of their members and leaders, and the size of the group they represent; and their connection with the process of financial allocation. To the extent that the agency is strong in each of these aspects it will be viewed as a political entity to be reckoned with, and its influence will therefore be heightened.

For many years, the University Grants Committee in Britain has been considered the paradigm of intermediate bodies for coordinating higher education systems. Structurally, it stands at the apex of the university sector, immediately below the government level. Moreover, it is national in scope but with a clear understanding of its purpose to represent university interests. Throughout the years since its statutory establishment in 1918, it has been manned by prominent academic figures whose influence was unquestionable.

Until recently, the UGC has held the decisive position on allocation of funds—just short of the Treasury. Now, however, another bureaucratic step has been inserted so that the UGC reports to the Department of Education and Science, which then conveys the matter to the Treasury. The added step is a vital one that has accordingly removed the UGC from its favored track and placed it no higher than the polytechnics and other institutional interests.

Still the UGC remains a model internationally. Australia has used its heritage effectively in this respect. Ontario began to do so in the 1960s when it set up a committee to receive financial requests from the universities and advise the Minister of Education on the amounts of annual grants. But, as financial expenditures increased, so did the government's concern for equitable distribution. Thus the Universities Committee became engrossed, together with the presidents of the Council of Ontario Universities, in devising mechanisms for formula financing.[22]

Equity in distribution is politically advantageous, but it may be educationally disadvantageous in the long run. It does not foster innovation or self-improvement; but rather supports the status quo syndrome. Formulas are based on built-in factors like the number of students at set levels of study or the physical space and facilities required. In such systems, the intermediate body's role naturally becomes less influential; it is less evaluative in judgment and, in practice, it tends to be merely another link in the chain of conveyance to the final authority.

The Ontario Committee on University Affairs has always been advisory to the minister, not determining, so it has not held the full prestigious command of Britain's UGC. Both France and Thailand have seriously studied adopting the British pattern, but neither has done so. No doubt it is just as well because imported patterns often fail to fit the lifestyle, customs, and needs of a different educational environment. Importation of an idea or concept works better and allows the pattern or form to be indigenously designed.

Intermediate bodies along the UGC model perform an important intermediary role—the negotiator—between their interest group and the government. Ontario originally viewed its university committee as the "buffer" that would give government "good and acceptable advice and also protect the universities from direct governmental intervention." Kymlicka sees this as the beginning of the search for an impartial agent to serve both sides.

> The quest, of couses, was for a mythical beast, though the myth that sustains it is a useful one and provides the necessary rhetorical justification for the institutions' reluctance to surrender whatever remains of their independence. By the same token, it allows the government to direct policies without being formally responsible for the consequences.[23]

It is a cynical point of view, not without reason when we recognize the powerful shift toward central government control. Intermediary bodies, however, have also a constructive role beyond self-protection for the opponents: they are educative in themselves and serve a communicative function between audiences that are frequently ill-informed regarding each other's purposes and concerns. This constructive role requires strengthening in all countries if higher education systems are to thrive and serve their societies. Adversarial positions are poor building blocks for cooperative structures, and they are equally weak in supporting coordination within systems.

The majority of intermediate bodies in higher education lack the actual power of statutory assignment and direct relationship to the process of financial allocation. Many are without binding power even over their own members. Yet they can be exceedingly influential, especially when their members hold high positions and their leadership is recognized. In these cases, the advisory function can take on the attributes of power, and recommendations of the group may be disregarded at the minister's peril.

In France, the Presidents' Conference "has grown over the years to the point where it now has a considerable—some would say excessive—effect on the system as a whole."[24] Similarly, Britain's Committee of Vice-Chancellors and Principals (CVCP) has lately developed a more active role in speaking publicly for their constituency. Foremerly, the UGC alone had the collective voice. But now, the CVCP has begun negotiations with students on participation and with university staff on salaries, and publishes collective views of the universities on major issues.[25]

The West German Conference of Rectors, which has long been the major spokesman for academic interests, functions as the counterpart to the Conference of Ministers of Education. Representing all higher education institutions at the teritary level, it works for collaboration of interests and specifically takes the objective of advising political decision makers in the legislative and executive branches of government.[26]

Many such voluntary bodies operate both within higher education systems and on the periphery of the more formal structure. Since "intermediate" includes innumerable levels between the top authority and the lowest groups, it encompasses a multitude of organizations and types.

Regardless of the detailed differences in the various countries' systems, intermediate groups naturally form themselves around positions held in the structural hierarchy and therefore interests commonly shared. Furthermore, it is axiomatic to note that the higher the position held, the broader the interests and the concerns will be. It is a matter of job definition, of responsibilities that accompany the positions. For example, committees of ministers must take the broadest view of all higher education under their jurisdiction; the next in line, committees of rectors, presidents, principals, or directors, are concerned primarily with institutions of their own type and the issues confronting their sector.

The following level of faculty tends to have more choices with limited interests. Faculty may be bimodal in representative bodies: one mode for their professional, intellectual association with colleagues of like specialty, and the other a collective bargaining agent for physical concerns of salary, benefits, and working conditions. They also have general membership in national associations of teachers which occasionally fulfill both the professional and personal functions. No matter how they divide or multiply their loyalties, there are ample voluntary associations to represent their interests.

Gradually the scope of concerns narrows so that clerical and lower administrative staff have membership available in state and national bodies representing their self-interests. Librarians, comptrollers and business officers, admissions directors, alumni directors, and others in some countries like the United States have comparable forums for exchange and discussion in their respective fields.

Students, as a transient community in higher education systems, do not fit in the more or less permanent structural levels of organization. After all, they are its purpose. Their issues may be as broad as those of general administrators or as narrow in self-interest as a bargaining group. Thus, their demands or recommendations usually appear before the higher governing groups of rectors and ministers.

There is a vast array of voluntary bodies existing in intermediate areas. Each of them, in one way or another, contributes to the coordination of the system; and all of them together complicate the administrator's life in the intricacies of management. In effect, he is asked to be the super-coordinator, the master negotiator among the groups, parleying demands and combining interests for a balanced and just administration that hopefully can move toward its goals.

Intermediate bodies located geographically on a regional basis form a more integral part of the structural organization of systems. They are usually administrative units established by law in the public systems that are typical of most countries. Creating smaller units dispersed regionally has been seen as a way to break up the centralized leviathan that some systems have become. Regional organization can be an effective tool for decentralization, but only if the geographic unit has a considerable share of autonomy and some role in financial allocation. Structure without power obviously accomplishes little more than a delivery system even though this can be beneficial in locating educational programs near the homes of students and in adapting courses to local needs. It does not, however, directly affect centralized control unless the control is actually shared. So, a system may *appear* decentralized on organizational charts, but it is not truly decentralized if central authority retains the vital decisions.

Two of the countries with most highly centralized, national systems have made deliberate moves toward decentralization through regional, intermediate bodies. France declared its intention in the Orientation Act of 1968; regional councils were to be established, along with measures to strengthen the presidency of universities, and to redistribute student enrollment. Decentralization, including increased autonomy for universities, was a major purpose of the legislation.

Today, some years later, evaluation shows limited success. Academic administration and presidencies are stronger, but student enrollment patterns have not changed significantly. And regional councils are a special story. According to the law (Title II, Article 8), the councils are comprised of elected representatives of the universities, of other institutions of higher education and research independent of the universities, and outside persons representing local governments and regional interests. Their functions are to contribute to planning and programming, and make recommendations to the national ministry on these aspects as well as requests for funds from the institutions. Moreover, coordination of the regional institution is a specific assignment.

Following the formal decree in 1972, members were elected, but the regional councils have never met. There is uncertainty over their role. The law, stated in general terms, left to the ministry the task of issuing decrees, regulations, and circulars to interpret and apply it. Summarizing the results, John Van de Graaff and Dorotea Furth conclude that the mission of the law has not yet been accomplished.

Paradoxically, at the national level, although most persons involved in drafting and implementing the Orientation Act favored decentralization, its implementation has reinforced ministerial control, at least in the short term.[27]

The French situation appears to be one in which a well-intentioned reform law has been derailed in its purpose, or at least sidetracked by long-established custom and by political factionalism.

Regional boards in Sweden were born from political conflict which began with the U68 commission. An idea that was dropped early in the commission's work, it was reintroduced in compromise to gain the support of the Center Party before the 1975 legislation. Not only would regional boards aid regional development, but they would provide places for more public representatives on boards.

The "public interest" was one of the most contested issues in the reform. So, if the public had only one-third of the seats on institutional governing boards, they would have two-thirds majorities on regional boards. Further, on the manner of appointment, the three nonsocialist parties won on having public representatives to institutional boards appointed by county and local authority councils rather than by central government which held its appointment rights for the regional boards.[28]

Of the 21 member boards, 14 represent the public while 6 come from higher education in the region. All are nominated by local, regional, and organizational interests that include two nominees from students of the institutions and three from the three big unions of Sweden, one each from the blue-collar and white-collar workers, and one from a union "almost unique to the Nordic countries"[29] which comprises professionals and others with higher education degrees.

The Swedish regional boards have progressed markedly, compared to the French boards' static situation, but not without considerable uncertainty over their functions and variation in their performance. Of the six regions, each with a university town as the "regional capital," the northern one is reported to be most active. But predictions vary greatly with regard to their future in the Swedish system.

Their tasks are similar to those projected in the Orientation Act for the French regional boards. They are responsible especially for overall planning to ensure diversified programs relating to regional needs. And for Sweden, it is important to know that regional boards serve not only state institutions, but also institutions under county authority and municipal councils. Theirs is a unitary role which is new. Administrative functions are few and the staff relatively small.

As part of their responsibility, the Swedish boards have the right to comment on institutional budget requests which must clear the regional level before going on to the National Board, a role that was also intended for the French boards. More specifically, however, the Swedish regional board is formally responsible for the allocation of funds for local and individual study programs and independent courses that add up to about 10 percent of the total funds for undergraduate education. The boards also have limited funds available for improving links between basic education and research, especially for educational institutions lacking such connections. The Swedish regional boards have a position in the budgetary process.[30]

It is too early to evaluate their importance or their future, but conjecture is a contagious game, enlivening the test of theories. In their first year of existence, after appointment in 1977, Rune Premfors reports that the environment was generally hostile and tension had developed between regional boards and the National Board of Universities and Colleges.[31] Some saw the regional boards becoming fairly powerful because of their political backing and the stature of the politicians on their boards (chairmen frequently have national reputations). But other observers predicted direly that the boards would fall into "a power vacuum between the traditionally strong forces at the central level and new, increasingly power-conscious local boards."[32]

Premfors takes a cautious position: the regional boards will last but be fairly powerless except in a few policy-making areas. The boards will not win out in budgeting; they will tend toward special concerns like distance education and the problems of weaker institutions located outside university towns; and their power will differ substantially among the six regions with the stronger boards emerging where the regions have less established universities.[33] In this opinion, at least, neither the universities nor the central authority is expected to alter significantly its customary position due to the regional boards' activities.

However, other reforms are also happening in the direction of decentralization, and many observers are surprised at the actual extent to which it is occurring. There are basic changes in the budgetary process, reducing the number of line items, grouping them into "planning frames" for programs, and allowing easier transference between line items. Increased autonomy concerns curricula and internal institutional structure as well. Universities have more "politicians" on their boards while nonstate institutions have program committees inserted between them and their governing boards. Extensive reforms are in progress.

There is no area of governance in higher education where shifts and changes take place as frequently as in the intermediate range. It is by far the most flexible stretch in the structural hierarchy: in practice, it serves as an experimental testing ground. Agencies are created and abandoned; and as super-agencies are installed, some bodies that were fomerly in the top echelon find themselves in the intermediate gray area. This will be true, for example, in the United States if state coordinating boards use their full powers. Or it is seen as the UGC in Britain accomodates its new position under the central department and as the Committee of Vice-Chancellors and Principals plays an increasing role representing the universities.

Similarly, as national authorities gain power in federally organized countries, the state or provincial level is thereby reduced to a regional, intermediate level in function, and it may gradually begin to show characteristics more like regional agencies set up by centralized systems in efforts to decentralize. But that is a rather long guess since provincial offices holding considerable power do not easily relinquish it. Instead, they are apt to wage a tug-of-war such as Canada and the Federal Republic of Germany are experiencing. Moreover, in the centralized country there is little inclination to share power to a significant extent with regional-level agencies. So the scene is transitional with situations shifting while the agencies come and go. At this point, a list of intermediate agencies in the 12 countries requires constant adjustment for additions and deletions.

Intermediate bodies have as many functions as types of organization. Coordination is a primary function, both regionally and within sectors of higher education systems, and the planning function accompanies it for most agencies. Fewer have specific administrative duties of any importance, except for those that perform managerially for sectors. The majority, including all the voluntary organized groups, have advisory roles in which recommendations are heeded according to the positions held by the members and the size of the group represented.

Thus far, the place where coordination is working best in systems is on the sectoral level. The boards or committees engaged structurally in the management of one of the several types of higher education—universities, colleges, technical institutes, and so on—are able to coordinate programs and activities more effectively than central authorities located farther away from the problems, interests, and personalities of the particular type of institutions. It argues obviously that coordination may be better achieved when done by those most familiar with what is being coordinated.

But this is only part of the job asked for. Legislative bodies increasingly want a *comprehensive* view of higher education for a total funding allotment as well as for evaluation of educational needs of the people. They want to see it working as a whole. To coordinate sectors and create a unified, comprehensive system of all higher education in a country is a formidable task when one considers the magnitude of the endeavor, the entrenched customs and loyalties of each segment and the wide differences among them, and the power centers stationed in various bureaucratic agencies.

The desirability of such a move may also be questioned in terms of possible outcomes. Regardless of the difficulties involved and the question of desirability, movement at present is toward coordination of the several sectors and toward arrangements to distribute higher educational opportunities more equitably with reference to geographic regions and students' interests. Organizationally, the trend is toward a unified system embracing all types of higher education. And with unification, more than likely, we will see growth in uniformity.

6
ACADEMIC AUTONOMY

Above all other aspects of higher education, academic autonomy in teaching and curricula is treasured, and rightly so. It is the essence of academic freedom and truth in the educative process. Our evidence shows that this, too, is changing; government policies are affecting academic autonomy more directly and specifically than in the past.

GOVERNMENT CONCERN

Higher education systems have increasingly become arms of social policy for their governments, which has led to increased attention and concern over higher education affairs. With the expansion in numbers of students, governmental budgets for higher education reached all-time highs; additional facilities have been provided, teachers added, new types of institutions founded, and student financial assistance increased. As the expansive cycle slowed and contraction set in with financial cutbacks, government concern was further sharpened. Add to this the economic problems in some countries of shrinking currencies and growing inflation, and there are ample reasons for closer government involvement in the affairs of higher education systems.

Moreover, political issues and society's problems have invaded campuses around the world and given additional impetus for government's entrance. The West German report aptly describes the situation:

> Because of the sometimes chaotic conditions at the universities, the excesses of the student movement, and the demand for new forms of university constitutions, the trend at universities, since the beginning of the

1970s, has been toward stronger governmental interference. This is reflected in the university laws of the Länder and in a wealth of regulations.[1]

Student demands for free speech and the right to be heard and participate in university governance have been vociferous and sometimes violent. The student movement circled the globe, appearing in Tokyo, Paris, New York, and Berkeley. In the United States, student uprisings on racial issues and the Vietnam War brought terrible consequences. Armed force was used and deaths occurred. Thailand and Iran have had university student leaders in political revolution. With the exceptions of Australia, Canada, and Sweden, where campus disorders and sever conflict have been less evident, each of our countries has seen violence and disruption in its universities.

Mexico had bloody fighting inside and outside the university. In the summer of 1977, federal police troops moved onto the campus of the National Autonomous University in Mexico City to quell the strike of faculty, administrative personnel, students, and university laborers. Yet the word "autonomous" appears in the name of the university, and it is included in the titles of most government universities in Mexico. A status conferred by law, it is intended to give the university general independence in handling its affairs. The status has been badly abused, and speculation since the riots has suggested

> ... legal modifications in the concept of autonomy, which could lead to the possibility of improvements in education, specifically to the imposition of some kind of academic criteria—including improved internal efficiency, both quantitative and qualitative—as a condition for the maintaining of autonomous status backed by government financial support.[2]

There would certainly be disagreement on the trade-off suggested for Mexico. As countries have experienced such disorders on various issues, public opinion toward the universities has been critical. Governments have been prompted not only to act on campuses, but to examine their systems of higher education with an eye toward reform.

Students have organized effectively in many countries, and formed student unions with considerable financial resources, particularly in Australia, Sweden, and the United Kingdom. As a consequence, their position on issues of debate and their participation in political processes have gained importance. They have been a strong element in the "politicization" of higher education and in attracting government notice to campus problems.

Substantial gains by student forces are apparent in their broader participation in the governing process of institutions and the higher education system. In France and the Federal Republic of Germany, student numbers on policy bodies have been significantly enlarged. They are less numerous in most countries on matters of faculty appointment and research. The

Anglo-Saxon countries and Japan have generally increased student representatives, but they are mostly advisory, without vote, on key academic committees.

While activism has slackened of late on specific issues in many countries, the student position has been established and has to be taken into account in university governance and in political affairs of the country. Students have formed a political constituency of influence that is new to the majority of the governments in our study. Along with economic and other social issues, student political involvement has resulted in greatly increased governmental attention to academic affairs.

Governments have long been *supportive* financially and socially for their systems of higher education; but the real issues is how *directive* they choose to be. Generally they have been cautious and restrained, and seldom have they chosen to exercise their full residual powers. Today, however, in each of our countries, government, whether central or provincial, is entering more actively into more areas of academic life.

AUTONOMY

For many years, the concept of autonomy—a state of independence in governance without outside control—was accepted, and governmental approvals were largely *pro forma*. There have been variations, of course, over time in almost every country, but usually governments have respected higher education's autonomous state. In the last decade or so, this has changed markedly; governments have increasingly made statements and, in some instances, laws and regulations that invade the so-called autonomy of institutions.

The word is no longer usuable in its true sense. One cannot correctly dissect *autonomy*; it either exists as independence of the institution in controlling its own affairs, or it does not. Lately, however, the word has been stretched in usage to apply to one or another specific activity of higher education systems. Because the existence of autonomy is diminishing, and educators are loathe to give up the past independence, they differentiate where and in what way autonomy still operates and where it is lost or threatened.

Following these distinctions, analysis shows government to be more operative and dominant in administrative matters—planning, regulations and structure for management, and coordination—than it is in curricular and program matters. But government's incursion into academic affairs is much more pronounced than is often realized.

The heart of academic autonomy lies in certain rights which are seen as the inheritance of professors and their institutions. While there are some differences among the countries' higher education systems, academic autonomy generally includes at least the first three of the following rights to:

- Teach one's subject as one knows it and sees it.
- Appoint and promote faculty.
- Choose and conduct research.
- Set standards for admission and graduation of students.

Government policies and actions are affecting these rights in a variety of ways that are both direct and indirect. Observations here concern the classroom, faculty, and curricula. Subsequent chapters discuss admissions and research.

CURRICULA AND FACULTY

The almost untouchable status of the classroom and the professor's prerogative in teaching his own subject in his own way have long been envied by those in other professions. Well-protected by his peers in the discipline, whether it was organized departmentally as in the United States or as a faculty in the European structure, the professor's position has been sacrosanct. And in the continental systems where he had, in addition, his own chair with the faculty built around him, he was doubly insulated.

Nonetheless, there are many means of affecting the classroom and the academic terrain, and governments are increasingly using them. The worldwide push for career and vocational training is an example of new demands on the classroom. Recent Swedish legislation asks that *all* higher education teach some type of vocational skill, and France's Orientation Law calls for "multidisciplinarity" in studies and the structural reorganization of faculties. Such laws closely affect the faculty's role and what they teach. Some governments, in particular West Germany, have asked that the length of time for higher study courses be reduced. Again, this asks for reorganization of subject matter.

Courses of study offered are increasingly determined by public policies. Government funds are given or withheld for particular programs depending on the needs of the society, as in the example of Japan. The British Department of Education and Science has closed a sizable number of teacher training colleges, and the majority of advanced nations are struggling with an oversupply of teachers and their training institutions, which will mean converting them to other types of curricula or closing them. There are, indeed, multiple paths to the classroom.

In many of the countries, curricular are directly subject to central office approval, which reaches the heart of autonomy in teaching. The Swedish report comments explicitly and cautions that practice may belie formal procedures:

> Decisions concerning curricula, by many considered to be at the core of institutional autonomy, were shown to be very centralized. Although the degree of centralization has varied between different parts of higher education, and even if formal procedures give an exaggerated view of the degree of centralization, this is probably the element which most concerns defenders of autonomy. In practice, central regulations have been eased successively since the late 1960s. The reform of 1977 has meant additional autonomy.[3]

West Germany is experiencing exactly the opposite trend: far from relaxing, government regulations regarding university curricula are tightening. One of the many points of current friction and controversy between institutions and the executive branch of government is the procedure by which "study regulations for all academic fields are approved."[4] The 1976 Frame Law for Higher Education limits the former freedom of teaching and learning which was characteristic of German universities. Under the law:

> The length of time a student should spend in a given course of study is to be defined and differentiated; study regulations are to be introduced that indicate courses and achievements a student must accomplish in order to complete his studies successfully....

> The emphasis on practice-orientation in the 1976 regulations indicates... that research, teaching, and studies are not to be confined to academic ivory towers and should instead be aimed more at professional and social demands.[5]

And the report concludes that the old euphoria of almost limitless freedom of "teaching through research" has yielded to a certain sobriety.

The German authors point out that planning specifications, though based on space requirements, directly influence classroom teaching and encourage the monologue of one-man lectures. Twenty types of teaching are distinguished in the second version of specifications. There are, indeed, many paths to classroom control, and one of the most lasting effects of planning regulations may well be the "bureaucratic control over the actual provision of teaching."

Government at both the federal and Länder levels is taking a stronger hand in academic matters. The movement is diametrically opposite to that of Sweden where government regulations are easing and autonomy has increased in recent reforms. Criticism by the German universities has been so great that broader evaluative guidelines, giving more autonomy to individual institutions, are to be issued in the future, but doubt exists over the extent of their improvement.

France, on the other hand, is in a muddled transition, a state of difficult ambivalence, between plans for decentralization of the system and resistance to change. The questionnaire used in the survey by Alain Bienayme concerning changes since the 1968 Orientation Law asked specifically for responses on two criteria defining academic autonomy: namely, the method of recruiting teaching personnel and the awarding of diplomas. Results show that respondents do not expect total latitude for universities either in recruiting personnel or in granting degrees. The demand for independence in standards for degrees is not strong; instead, flexibility is desired in procedures and requirements for both. The author observes that "professors, although they favor the concept of autonomy, want to keep the umbrella of their civil status." And even those who approve national diplomas want more freedom to determine requirements because the central government ministry is making decisions "on new degree programs with inadequate information as to what is actually happening within the universities."[6]

On hiring teachers, the Swedish report repeats its point that formal centralization is obvious in the regulations, but the real decision making occurs much lower down in the hierarchy—among the peer group. Again in opposition, West Germany expresses its anxiety over the interference in appointments by ministers of culture. Approval is no longer merely a formal procedure.

In these three countries—France, Sweden, and West Germany—faculty are civil servants as they are also in Thailand and Poland. Their tenure is assured, but their obligations must also be affected. They have two masters: government and the ideal of autonomy. It is a schizophrenic combination theoretically, but such trade-offs are not unfamiliar in the life of man. The dilemma, however, has generally been solved through restraint on the part of government bulwarked by public opinion. The tradition of academic freedom is strong, but it may well be asked whether its position is eroding and whether academics who have used their freedom negatively have not contributed to its weakening position.

INSTITUTIONAL DIFFERENCES

Traditionally, universities with research and high level studies have been ouside the scope of direct approval for courses and curricula; they have been given the freedom in their internal affairs that characterizes autonomy. Other institutions, however, within systems of higher education have not had such unrestricted status. In Sweden, a large share of higher education institutions are under the direct authority of regional and local bodies. Comparable in this respect are the polytechnics in Britain and the community colleges in the United States. Institutions serving their immediate communities by offering practical curricula—and benefiting from local financial support in some instances—are more closely tied to their sources of support and therefore generally enjoy less autonomy in curricular matters as well as administrative affairs.

The same holds true for institutions directly responsible to one or another ministry of government. Most frequently agricultural institutes, military academies, and sometimes programs in health services are specifically under the appropriate government agency. In these cases, relationships are close, and supervision of curricula and institutional management is not at all unusual.

Though universities have been favored and allowed to go their own way, especially in academic affairs, compared to other types of institutions in the systems, this preferred status is diminishing. The United States provides extraordinary examples of new controls on university curricula. In New York State, the Board of Regents (elected by the legislature) ordered some 24 doctoral programs of the State University shut down because of low quality, and their decision was upheld in the court; the Louisiana regents closed 18 doctoral programs for the same reason; and a Tennessee court ruled that a doctorate program at the Graduate School of Management at Vanderbilt University was inadequate and hastily conceived, and students were to be refunded their fees. (The Vanderbilt program was later improved.) While such drastic actions are relatively few in number, they are appearing with increasing frequency, especially court judgements in cases brought by students as consumers or by faculty charging discrimination or unfair practices if they have failed to be retained or to be granted tenure.

The majority of states in the United States have general statutes or regulations of a rather vague and undemanding nature pertaining to curriculum and faculty qualifications for public degree granting institutions. Some states have licensing and oversight statutes and regulations of similar type dealing with course length, content, and objectives for private institutions. Only in the last few years have such issues become prominent and then it has usually been a question of maintaining quality and protecting against abuse.

The increasing power of coordinating and central governing boards, described earlier, means that review of academic programs is now more prevalent. Some even control program content, i.e., courses. Private institutions are not necessarily exempt. For example, New York's Regents, acting as a coordinating board, must approve any new curricular program before it can be given by a private liberal arts college. And the college must show that its program will not duplicate another already offered by a nearby institution.

Federal regulations on academic programs have not existed on specific grounds until recently when they were tied to financial aid, especially for veterans; they were designed to curb abuses.

Nevertheless, on a general basis, federal aid has gone only to institutions "accredited" in their academic programs by the regional network of cooperative accrediting associations throughout the country. The issue now is whether the regional organizations will take stronger positions in criticism of faulty programs and abuses or whether this will be done by the courts and further governmental regulations. Many hope for self-regulation and voluntary measures rather than external controls, but the outcome is uncertain.

Universities in Ontario, Canada, have been in a comparable situation regarding appraisal of new Ph.D. programs. The Ontario Council on Graduate Studies was unable to enforce participation of institutions, so the government stepped in and "proclaimed tht it would not fund any new Ph.D. (or, for that matter, master's) programs if they did not successfully pass the appraisal procedure."[7] This action spoke forcefully to the universities, all financed on a formula basis by public funds. Later, an Advisory Committee on Academic Planning was added to assess development of discipline groups and coordinate graduate studies in the province. Ontario has cooperative arrangements between academics and the government Ministry of Colleges and Universities, but the overall shift has been toward greatly increased powers in government.

European countries have long had more formal controls over their higher education systems than, for example, Canada and the United States. Those controls included approval of academic courses and faculty appointments. The European systems were accustomed to such procedures and to their full financial support from government. There was no serious lack of autonomy in teaching and curricular affairs. The powerful position of professors saw to that, and academics usually staffed government offices that dealt with academic affairs. They understood the attitudes and ways of the academic enterprise.

Today, however, the professor's position is greatly weakened, the administrative echelon is strengthened, and academic personnel have less influence in the ministry for higher education. Customs are changing with the new forces and factors that have come into play. Thus the French and German reports express higher education's worry over government actions that impinge on academic autonomy.

Through decentralization of the system Sweden is trying to encourage autonomy and initiative in local and regional areas. It is an effort to counter the centralization and uniformity that pervades the higher education system, including its curricular and academic aspects. However, other external forces may play a more dominant part and affect institutional autonomy in different ways under the reform in progress. These external influences are discussed in Chapter 9.

With the exception of Sweden—and perhaps Mexico where the trend academically is unclear—the governments of the 12 countries are generally moving toward tighter reins and an increasing presence in academic affairs. In many ways the trend is inevitable. The old freedom to teach what, how, and when one wished was too costly.

7
ADMISSION POLICIES AND ACCESS

In the view of many, admission policies are closely tied to academic autonomy since entrance standards affect the level and quality of instruction. Such an attitude, for example, is strongly held in the United States private sector. Faculty insist not only on approving admission policies, but also on screening applicant dossiers to be sure policies are adhered to. The attitude is also found in some highly selective public universities though the majority are acustomed to having admission policies set by the state.

For the great majority of higher education systems, government's position in determining admission policies is thoroughly established and expected. There is certainly nothing new in government's legitimate concern over who and how many will receive higher education. The change is rather in the enormous extension of its supportive role and the increased use of directive policies. As many students who formerly would have been unable to attend higher education institutions were admitted, governments encouraged expectations and demand for entrance; and costs escalated. Naturally government surveillance of higher education's activites increased and more policies and rules were added.

EXPANSION OF PLACES

To cope with the public demand and numbers of students applying, governments have generally followed three steps, and most of them have stopped, or at least rested, on the third step. However, five governments—Poland, the United States, West Germany, Sweden, and, to a lesser extent, Thailand—have proceeded to the next step which involves closer controls and the concept of quotas, if not actually designated percentages or numbers.

The general approach has been:

1. Expansion of facilities and places for students by duplicating universities and colleges. This is "more of the same," since expansion merely reflected the existing pattern—more places, but neither new programs nor diversification for new audiences.
2. Creation of new types of institutions and courses to serve the broader needs of both society and the students. On this step, the United States, Canada, and Japan started community and two-year colleges. In some instances, countries transformed existing institutions into new types with different purposes, as Britain's polytechnics and West Germany's *Fachhochschulen.*

   In all cases, vocational and technical education—practical training—has received additional impetus and funds.

   Accompanying this stage are relaxed entrance standards—compared to selective universities and colleges—and more adults have entered higher institutions, sometimes with credit for work experience.
3. The declaration of "open admissions" to provide further access for many students. Graduation from the secondary school is still expected in the open admission of many states in the United States, as it is in France for university entrance, in Thailand for the open Ramkhamhaeng University, and so on.

   For the Open University in Britain, however, a secondary school diploma is not required; courses are truly open except for the age stipulation and ability to pay the relatively modest cost for courses. No model has been so rapidly copied, and its further promise is great. At the moment, it signifies the ultimate in the trend toward open admission practices.

   Similarly, more institutions in the various countries are using the words "or its equivalent" when stating entrance requirements with regard to diplomas. Sweden has lowered formal education requirements in the "25:4" program which allows adults 25 years of age and over who have been gainfully employed (housewives included in the definition) for 4 years to enter. In the new reform program they need only a minimum knowledge of English corresponding to a two-year course in upper-secondary school. Special qualifications, however, are needed for some study programs.

The three steps noted have been taken in the broad sense in all the countries. While they provide greatly increased numbers of places for students, and admission policies have been adjusted accordingly, these steps do not satisfy the criteria of choice among institutions, nor do they fully solve the problem of elitism. They merely offer more opportunities, usually along *one* or another line. Talent and ability may still be bound by the location of a home, the family income, and the number of places available in specific fields.

QUOTAS

In an age of egalitarianism, some governments have judged these measures inadequate and so have instituted quotas or adopted policies that imply quotas. The policy is simple and clear in Poland: "Political directives—formulated in laws, acts, and regulations—provide for a stable percentage of students from manual workers' and peasant families in institutions of higher education."[1] Following a careful sorting out process from the primary grades on, the effort is made to find and prepare the best candidates. Although the process is naturally subject to human imperfection and the categories admittedly difficult to define, the percentages among those newly enrolled in higher education in 1976 indicate a fairly successful system: 31.9 percent from workers' families; 10.4 percent from peasant families; 54.5 percent from the intelligentsia; and 3.2 percent from other classes. Workers and peasants' children are entering higher education in considerable numbers—42.3 percent together. If *graduates* of that same year are counted, percentages indicate 49.3 percent from worker and peasant families. The attrition rate runs higher for the intelligentsia.

Quotas, of course, are anathema in the United States, but it may as well be admitted that while the word is abhorred, federal government policies, in fact requirements, call for similar results. Attempting to redress social inequity, the government has embarked on an "affirmative action" policy which asks for increases in the numbers of minority persons and women in both admission practices and appointment practices for faculty and administrators. The disputed question is "reverse discrimination" or "benevolent quotas" which favor the minority in admissions—sometimes at the expense of white males with superior records.[2] In practice, quotas have frequently been set by institutions to reserve places, especially for minorities, and sometimes for women, in the latter case particularly in programs that customarily included only a few or no women.

Evidence of affirmative action is required of private institutions as well as public; the "axe" hanging over the institutional head is the withdrawal of federal funds, and it has been used in threatening actions and actual withdrawal—even in the case of a private institution like Columbia University—until the condition is bettered. Most institutions have worked hard to find and attract qualified minority students, adding remedial programs where necessary; and the enrolled numbers of such students have greatly increased. The effort has been worthwhile and endorsed by most institutions and the public generally—up to a point.

That point seems to have been reached recently in the Bakke case, in which a white male student sued a public university for discrimination favoring black students in medical school entrance. The Supreme Court held that Bakke must be admitted; that race, nevertheless, is a proper factor in admissions decisions; but quotas as a means of providing places for minority students were specifically rejected. Although the ruling is ambiguous, it is interpreted as sustaining affirmative action.

The argument continues between those who think not enough is being done to aid the disadvantaged and others who consider government actions an infringement of basic individual rights. No one disputes that it is the area into which the federal government—legislature, courts, and executive branch—has entered most forcefully, and with the most far-reaching results for higher education.

Quotas came into the new Swedish system of higher education on a nationwide, uniform scale with general requirements and selection rules fixed by the *Riksdag* and refined by the Cabinet. Besides the obvious egalitarian principle, there is the assumption "that real competence should be the deciding factor, not formal education." Moreover, positive discrimination on social criteria can be practiced by local boards judging individual cases. The intricate complications of the quota system are apparent in the quotation.

> The new system of admission introduces a complicated procedure by which applicants are divided into four quota groups. The groups get places in relation to their relative size. They are: (1) applicants with three years of *gymnasium* education; (2) applicants with two years of *gymnasium* education; (3) applicants from "folk high schools;" and (4) other applicants (namely, "25:4 applicants"). There is also a fifth group: applicants with foreign education. However, they are not allotted places in proportion to their applications but are, rather, competing for a predetermined number of places (not exceeding 10 percent of the total).
>
> Applicants in groups 1 and 2 are ranked according both to school marks and work experience. However, 20 percent of the places in these groups are allotted only according to marks. Applicants in group 3 . . . are ranked following a special assessment obtained from their schools.
>
> Finally, applicants in group 4 are ranked according to the combined value of work experience and the result of a voluntary aptitude test. The test is general in character and is supposed to tell whether an applicant is capable of pursuing higher studies.[3]

It should be observed that there are still special requirements that vary for different programs or courses, and these are set either by the central agency or local bodies.

The new Swedish procedure is quite different from past practices which were more traditional in asking the certificate from formal upper-secondary school. Under the old plan, sutdents chose between the unrestricted "free faculties" (humanities, social and natural science, theology, and law) and the *numerus clausus* or restricted faculties. For the latter, marks were the decisive factor in acceptance. Since the fall of 1979, all students apply for study lines and single subjects, with the quota formula applicable only for fields of limited enrollment. But, in the new plan the overwhelming number of study programs are restricted, so the quota system will be extensively used.

Modifications had been tried since the late 1960s, and at least two ad hoc commissions had made recommendations. Throughout the process, political decisions were fairly unanimous; "only the Conservative Party and a small minority of academics have had serious doubts about the general policy content of the new system."[4]

West Germany, on the other hand, has little agreement—only severe controversy over admission policies and the even more complicated formulas devised for fair consideration of applicants. German students with the *Arbitur* (certificate of successful completion of secondary studies) have characteristically been free to enter the university of their choice. And most important, the right to a place for higher study and the free choice of a profession are expressly guaranteed in the Basic Law of the Federal Republic.

Hence, when *numerus clausus* was used to cope with the overwhelming numbers of applicants, legal suits began charging violation of the right. In 1972, the Federal Constitutional Court—not unlike the United States Supreme Court—ruled in a general manner. Reaffirming the basic right, *numerus clausus* for new students in constitutional only:

> If it is kept within absolutely necessary limits and if the existing educational capacities supported by public means are utilized to their maximum;

> If appropriate criteria are applied to select students and to assign them to specific universities so that every qualified applicant has a chance and his personal choice of university may be considered.[5]

Following the court order, the eleven Länder, each with its own system of higher education, set up a central agency, country-wide in scope, for student placement.

The agency selects students for *numerus clausus* fields by applying "achievement and aptitude" criteria based on the grade average of the *Arbitur* and "time of waiting." After deducting special quotas for foreigners and hardship cases, 60 percent of students are admitted on achievement and 40 percent on waiting time. Remarking on the maze of instructions and questionnaires, Peisert and Framhein suggest that "properly filling out these forms could in itself be interpreted as proof of the student's 'maturity' for university."[6]

More dissatisfaction centers on the significance ascribed to grades from the secondary school. In 1976, the Frame Law added regulations for the fields requiring an especially high grade average or having particularly long waiting periods. In these fields there are to be supplementary tests and practical experience is to be taken into account.

Another stipulation of the law is far harder to carry out and more fraught with difficulties. To solve disparities in requirements of secondary schools and in grading among the eleven Länder, the Frame Law calls for "Länder quotas for the selection of student applicants as long as an equivalence of requirements and grading has not been established among the Länder." The Land quota is set at one-third of its applicants and two-thirds of its proportion of 18- to 21-year-olds among the population of the Land. Ministers of Culture intend to achieve standardized requirements through introduction of "norm books," which in effect represent a "centralistic and rigid intervention in the structure of curricula of secondary schools."[7]

Finally, in the midst of these various diabolic schemes, the government heads of the Bund and Länder met in November 1977, and resolved "to open up universities." Results are that the central agency assigns students in only 12 courses of study and this number will be further limited to the most crowded fields in the future; moreover, universities are to receive students above and beyond the available study spaces with the criterion being a 15 percent overcharge to alleviate the situation somewhat. The authors conclude that this policy to open up universities must confuse the public as it accompanies a growing number of applicants and stagnant personnel capacities. Critics therefore argue that by this policy "the devil of admission restrictions" is driven out by the "Beelzebub of nonfunctioning universities."[8]

Thailand's use of quotas is mere child's play compared to the complexities in West Germany and Sweden. The Thai system simply limits teacher-training college admissions to students living within the "college boundary," which helps guarantee provincial equality for entrance. And each college's quota is based on the proportion of the population living within its boundary. Also, to serve regions more equitably, in the fourth national plan, Khon Kaen, Chieng Mai, and Prince of Songkla universities have target quotas set, respectively, at 25, 30, and 40 percent for local students from the combined provinces in their regions.[9]

MARKET DEMAND

Quotas as a means of allocating places that are necesarily restricted for students may bring innumerable problems, arguments, and unforeseen inequities, but what happens in systems that are open to secondary school graduates on the basis of market demand? The selection process can become equally absurd at times, troublesome, and subject to manipulation and students may not fare any better.

Japan's system of higher education faces problems of magnitude equal to that of the Federal Republic of Germany, if not as complicated. Far from detailed quotas or lottery numbers, Japan's is an "intellectual horse race," in which the training starts in kindergarten, and the stakes are high—even life itself for some applicants. Known as *shiken jigoku* ("exam hell") it is a fierce competition that, until 1978, meant taking separate examinations for each university and, on average the year before, a student took five such examinations.[10]

A common examination for national and public universities has now been instituted: it is an objective, computer-scored achievement test based on secondary school education. Students, however, will continue to take separate examinations in the spring for the university(ies) of their choice, and combined scores on the two will determine admissions. Presumably universities will use scores on the common test to decide those eligible for the separate exam. "Hell" will not disappear; it will only be encountered less frequently. No doubt the business enterprises that have developed cram courses, special predictive examinations, and so on will continue their high profits.

The extreme competition, which results in heightened suicide rates among young people, has its roots in the society itself. The problem is not insufficient places for students in Japan; in 1975, of those applying 69.9 percent were admitted, an average entrance competition of 1.43 which is not excessive. Private institutions especially have been established to serve the many applicants, but their standards are generally not so high as the traditional, prestigious, and steeply graded national universities. It should be mentioned that "quotas" have been set for private higher institutions in an effort to control overall growth. These, however, are total limits and do not appear to involve detailed admission practices for individual students. The problem, instead, stems from society's system of awards, the Japanese attitude toward the job a person holds and the company which guarantees his position economically and socially. Hence, the degree from the "right" university, which means appointment to the desirable company, is the student's passport to a station in life.

Another pernicious competition appears in come private professional schools of medicine and dentistry where applicants donated an average of about $56,000 and $42,000 respectively for admission in 1977. "In general, the lower the entrance examination scores, the greater the amount of money the applicants must donate."[11] Of course, the practice is widely criticized in Japan, but it is obvious to what lengths such fanatical competition can go. Furthermore, the practice is not unheard of elsewhere: in the United States there have been charges of payments to institutions for admission, especially to medical schools, and the practice is feared to be more widespread than officials care to admit.

One comparative observation is in order. While Japan has a deeply imbedded "pecking order" for its universities, West Germany pointedly reminds us that no such hierarchy exists among its universities. In general, they are considered to be of equal standing, which is in marked contrast to Western countries, Thailand, Japan, and most places. This attitude undoubtedly assists the quota system in West Germany where a student may be assigned to any university having the appropriate field of study. Furthermore, the authors say that universities are not in competition to get the best students according to entrance examinations.[12]

It is difficult for the foreign observer to believe that such equality reigns among universities and that they are not considered to have differences in status. Britain has claimed academic equivalency of university degrees, but certainly the international reputations of Oxford and Cambridge elevate the value of their degrees to graduates. Competition for entrance has to be more difficult than at the redbrick universities and other institutions, just as it is tougher at Ivy League and other prestigious universities, public as well as private, in the United States.

Between the countries with the extremes of tight quotas and open market demand fall the remainder of the higher education systems, each with its own variety of admission problems. In France, the universities have dealt with the burden of mass enrollments on an open basis, while the *grandes écoles* remain highly selective, thus creating a binary system with problems not yet adequately confronted. Mexico has absorbed a 286 percent enrollment increase in a little over ten years. The system lacks standard procedures of any sort, and reforms are urgently needed.

Prerevolutionary Iran was similar in the need for systematic procedures to cope with the tremendous demand, which far exceeded places and forced many students to go abroad for further education. Work had progressed on standards for selection of students, and, although the process was still far from adequate, the secondary school grade average had been added to the national admissions test score in evaluating students.

Thailand's admission practices are closer to the more developed countries and particularly Japan, but fortunately Thailand does not seem to have such severe competition among students, even though applicants far outnumber those accepted. At present, in addition to the open policies at Ramkhamhaeng which admits secondary school graduates without further tests, applicants generally take a joint examination for ten of the government universities and institutes, and selective examination in some instances. Private colleges, with the reputation of taking anybody who applies, have become more selective and administer their own entrance tests.

On the whole the United States has been fortunate in having a wide diversity of institutions, both in types and entrance standards, scattered across the country. States determine admissions criteria for their own public systems. In some instances, state coordinating boards set minimum admission standards and establish ceilings on enrollment, institution by institution or by segments. Private institutions control their own selection process.

Affirmative action for minorities and women marks the beginning of direct policy intervention by the federal government in admission policies. Before this action, the federal role affected numbers of students and aid to the lower income levels, but did not specify any particular group for special consideration in admissions.

Australia, Canada, and the United Kingdom have managed to accept larger numbers of students, primarily through the development of additional institutions and types of programs in which barriers of qualification are not so high as in the universities that continue to be autonomous in their own admission. Nevertheless, the higher education systems in these countries and others in the study face many unsolved problems in adjusting to enrollment demand from students with more diverse backgrounds if higher education is to become equal in opportunity.

At the same time, enrollments of the typical college-age group are expected to decline in many advanced countries. Policies and rules will shift again, and enrollment-driven formulas for financial support will have to be reevaluated. Otherwise, higher education systems may be seriously hurt in the quality and diversity of their programs. Expanding enrollments for adults may ease the decline if policies favoring their admission and studies are further enacted. Such possibilities are considered in Chapter 9.

Viewed over the last 20 years, it is impossible to conceive of the tremendous growth that has occurred in higher education without the dominant push from government and its accompanying financial support. For a multitude of political, social, and economic reasons, governments have high stakes in access policies and admission criteria. Their concerns are generally over the equity of standards and the breadth of opportunities provided for citizens.

Purely academic criteria for admission are being challenged; more realistic standards are sought, as in Sweden's recognition that admission should be based on real competence, not formal education, and the United States practice of given academic credit based on experience outside the classroom. Admission tests, whether based on achievement or aptitude, are highly criticized for the limited range of abilities tested and the monopoly they frequently hold over standards for entrance.

Many adjustments lie ahead for higher education systems as they seek to accomodate a broader clientele. Moreover, government interests are intricately entwined, through control of access policies, with higher education's future.

8
RESEARCH

In the research function of higher education systems, government's role is absolutely vital; it is crucial as the prime source of funds and as the major determinant of allocation policies. The issues concerning research raised by the country reports, however, are considerably more complicated than simply the changes in government position, important as they are. Questions are discussed in some instances that reach into the nature of research itself and into the basic concept of unity in teaching and research which has long been the distinguishing hallmark of the university. Although the issues are closely intertwined, we will first examine the scene in government from the university's point of view and then relate other aspects of the research picture in these countries around the world. Universities are singled out from systems as a whole in this discussion since they, rather than the colleges and vocational post-secondary institutions, are the home of research.

As part of general financial difficulties and shifts in priorities, some governments are giving less to research or, at best, they are holding the amount steady. More legislative bodies are reviewing research programs and the process of making awards. In the last few years, several have established differentiated research councils for the allotment process in social sciences and humanities, natural sciences, medicine, and engineering research. Examples are Canada and Sweden; each has set up three such councils largely composed of academic researchers to make the allotments.

Following the centralized pattern, France, in contrast, has a single council to coordinate all research in the country except for atomic energy. The council allocates public funds for all agencies, of which higher education is simply one.

Beyond trends toward closer scrutiny and sometimes reduction in amount, the grants for university research must be seen in relation to the total government expenditure for research. How much are universities getting compared to other research agencies in the country? Is the balance changing? This is where analysis reveals a new development, one that could be immense in its implications for universities as well as higher education systems.

SPECIALIZED CENTERS

Government contracts for research are going, with increasing frequency, to specialized research institutes or centers other than universities. Four of our countries indicate the trend, and in the fifth—Japan—it does not involve a change, but a situation that already exists. Jan Szczepański comments on Poland where *outside* institutes receive more and more money compared to universities. "The Polish Academy of Sciences now has almost 70 research institutes, primarily conducting basic and statistical research, and development institutes linked directly to various ministries and engaged mostly in applied research."[1] Furthermore, the research employees have faculty status and titles but do not teach.

West Germany reflects the same situation with respect to big science establishments outside the universites: it has the Max Planck Society with 51 institutes and the Frauenhofer Society with 29 institutes for applied technological research. The United States report recognizes the increased competition from outside, independent centers like Rand Corporation, Brookings Institution, Bell Laboratories, and so on, but this does not suggest that universities are yet basically affected in their grants for research. There is simply the intimation that they may be so affected in the not too distant future.

The French report claims that research monies are not distributed with any definite policy between the central institutes for research and the universities, which are on the losing ends of awards. In Japan, universities do not have a significant role in research, and the authors specifically mention the need to rectify this.

So it would appear that some of the leading countries in the economic world are moving much research to specialized centers or have already placed it there. From the standpoint of governments, the shift to specialized centers may make sense, and to many voters it may appear in the same light. No doubt such centers are easier to control in reporting, and they provide a means of centralizing specialized projects with the expensive equipment required; and full-time work from researchers is possible.

From the universities' position, however, in the countries where the shift is occurring, what are the implications? They are expected both to help create advanced knowledge and to teach it. Szczepański states explicitly and very strongly the possible effects on the purpose and functions of universities:

Scientific discoveries and developments are now pursued in many research institutions outside higher education, so the universities have lost their monopoly as research institutions. This gives rise to many doubts about the purpose of the universities, especially since there is the real danger that the universities will lose contact with the real progress in science; at present, the most sophisticated research—such as that linked with outer space exploration—is being done in military institutions. Industry is also conducting very advanced research, and the results are generally classified and unknown in the institutions of higher education. Under these conditions, even attempting to measure the effectiveness of teaching in the transmission of new scientific knowledge can be questioned. What is the significance of academic freedom in the universities when the research conducted in military and industrial institutions is under very strict control? What is the purpose of university education when some groups of managers and highly qualified personnel are trained in business institutions and when the political elite is formed within political parties? Are the universities becoming only institutions that educate students who cannot find employment after graduation? It is from this perspective that the problems of effectiveness become really important.[2]

The separation of advanced research from the university would not only revolutionize the concept of higher education, but it would deeply affect expectations for the faculty and, of course, the financial support of institutions themselves. More vital still would be the effect on the next generation's leaders if universities cannot instruct them in advanced knowledge that is imprisoned in research laboratories located elsewhere.

Sweden, in contrast to Poland, West Germany, France, the United States, and others, has deliberately not created highly specialized research centers outside the universities. Hence, of the total allotment for research from the government through the research councils, some 70 percent goes to universities and other institutions in higher education. Additional funds are awarded by central agencies to higher education institutions for research and development activities. The percentage is very different in other countries.

Of the total expenditure for research and development, Australian universities receive about 20 percent, and Canadian universities get about 17 percent. Even though it is difficult to know the accuracy of the base in figuring such percentages, it is safe to conclude that industry and government-sponsored research are receiving larger shares. The specialized and classified nature of much research today may inevitably lead in this direction.

West German universities are awarded 30 percent of the total with industry at 47 percent, and outside research centers at 19 percent. Last year in the United States, nearly half of all federal funds for basic research went to universities, but it must be remembered that funds are concentrated at some 50 universities that receive the largest amounts. The narrowing focus toward specialized centers continues, whether outside or within the university sector.

APPLIED VERSUS BASIC

A second major shift that demands thoughtful attention from systems of higher education is the move toward applied research. Accompanying the pragmatic age and the concern for vocational-career education comes the emphasis on short-term projects that show evidence of practical results, and the test of truth in its immediate consequences. Some loss is to be expected in long-range principles and advanced learning.

Sweden states the issue in connection with grants made by central agencies. More and more researchers are accepting this type of "sectoral research money" which, critics say, leads to narrowly applied research—often with political strings attached to it—at the expense of basic research and a disinterested quest for truth. Critics of these grants charge invasion of academic freedom but, as the author reminds them, sectoral research funds are not vital to the survival of the discipline and so can be refused by those who feel their integrity is being compromised. Furthermore, he adds, the diversity of sources for research funds should be viewed as an asset.[3]

Lyman Glenny, speaking for the United States, sees too much money going into specific, short-term projects, and suggests that funding agencies reflect their governments in wanting to produce results to solve concrete problems of social priority.[4] Much discussion goes on in the United States about science policies, government regulations and red tape, and inadequate continuity in funding basic research. Arguments on the definition of basic versus applied research may complicate financial statements, but the trend toward applied projects has been unmistakable.

THE NATURE OF RESEARCH

Beyond the current emphasis on applied research, questions are being raised in many countries about the purpose and the desirability of some research. More than the cost factor has become formidable; there are inherent dangers in some types of scientific research such as genetic engineering and recombinant research which require legal safeguards and protection of human subjects. Complex questions arise concerning nuclear research and development. These and other issues have brought the public onto campuses in demonstrations, and they have brought governments into a more active role. Tony Becher, in the United Kingdom's report, mentions the new debate on the merits and demerits of research projects which is now underway, and he observes: "It is no longer possible for academics to indulge without let or hindrance in the time-honoured activity of pursuing truth."[5]

Indicating the troubled times for university research in the United States, Alan Pifer comments on the present inadequacy of the rationale that advanced research is essential to the nation's defense. The argument "runs into strong post-Vietnam feelings that universities should keep clear of anything to do with the military—even though research and how it is used are obviously two very different things." On the domestic front, he continues:

> The argument that high-level research and training in the universities are essential to the solution of major domestic problems and to the general social and economic progress of the nation runs into widespread skepticism today. It even encounters in some groups, especially among some young people, an antagonism, based on moral grounds, to the very idea of 'progress.'[6]

Many of these feelings are worldwide among the young, and the not so young. Similar attitudes are reflected among environmentalists and by the conservation movement not bounded by country borders. It is natural that universities are both involved and affected by such public sentiments.

TEACHING AND RESEARCH

The changing nature of research itself and the questions being asked, the high costs, and the shifts toward specialized institutions and toward applied research—all have affected the established concept of the basic unity of teaching and research in the university. Since the beginning of the nineteenth century, Humboldt's rationale for teaching through research has dominated European universities and those in the English-speaking world.

In Poland, where the concept was adopted early, it appears to endure as an undeviating principle for universities. Throughout the Polish report, adherence to the concept is emphasized, which may well be one reason why the trend to remove research from universities to the Polish Academy is so strongly contested by Szczepański.

The reports on the less developed countries of Iran, Thailand, and Mexico indicate not only their acceptance of Humboldt's concept, but their desire to achieve it as a goal long overdue. It is true that the professor's active research and knowledge of methodology will raise the quality of instruction, but these countries—before they emulate the more advanced nations—would be wise to examine the present stages of adjustment in those nations with regard to the research–teaching syndrome.

In Humboldt's homeland of Germany, where the doctrine held for more than a century and fashioned the university style, it is now challenged. Under the Federal Republic's Frame Law:

> ...there is no longer any insistence upon the unity of research and teaching in the strict, classical sense. The ratio between research, teaching, and studies remains open. It is only defined insofar as the institutions, in cooperation with government agencies, are given the permanent task to develop and adjust the contents and form of studies to new developments in science and art and also to the changing needs of the professional world.[7]

The statement applies to all higher institutions, including universities. The marriage of teaching and research has lost its sanctity and unquestioned allegiance; the relationship is weakened and broadened to recognize other means of achieving new knowledge and instructing students.

Sweden has followed a more direct route toward separation of teaching and research, and started on it earlier. During the 1960s, many colleges were created or elevated into university-type institutions, but they lacked research facilities and were not expected to combine research with teaching. This was especially true of university branches established in 1967: they were to concentrate solely on undergraduate teaching. So a considerable body of higher institutions developed without research, which was left to the more traditional universities.

Over the years, however, in the universities, research was separating out at the postgraduate level. Since the 1950s, the preponderant amount of teaching has been done by full-time lecturers.

> Increasingly, the teachers of postgraduate students have been separated from their colleagues at the undergraduate level: two subsystems are said to have emerged within academic departments.[8]

So the separation of research from teaching has not only been between types of institutions but within the university itself. The pattern of the past that expected all universities to offer "research-based" education with academics dividing their time between research and teaching has been broken. The authors consider the separation now a characteristic feature of higher education in Sweden.

The Swedish experience is not unique. As the authors recognize, many advanced nations have seen the same or similar developments: first, in the establishment of new types of higher institutions without the research function, and second, in the segregation of research at the graduate or postgraduate level, which frequently creates a division in the academic department.

Separation of teaching and research seems to be anticipated in Japan even as the need to raise the standards and increase the amount of scientific research is recognized. The Basic Guidelines for the Reform of Higher Education reaffirm the importance of research in the graduate school but point out that it has become impossible for professors to conduct high-level research and at the same time teach large numbers of students.

> Faced with the conflicting demands for education and research, it is feared that reliance on the traditional conception of the university, in which education and research activities are inseparable, will result in both activities being inadequately handled. It is important, therefore, to differentiate the roles and functions of educational institutions, taking into account their aims, character and internal organization, in accordance with the different requirements of education and research.[9]

Although the growing separation is a reality, university faculty in the more developed countries are still expected to combine the two functions. The principle is a bit of academic mythology that persists in a tenacious way. It pervades the atmosphere and clouds the view of reality. Tony Becher, in the report from the United Kingdom, confronts the myth surrounding research and focuses a clear light on the concept of research. He points out that "research is in practice by no means as universal a pursuit in higher education as was traditionally believed," and part of the reason lies in definition.

> There is a common tendency, in discussing academic research, to have in mind the physical scientist in his specialist laboratory.... The lone mathematician solving an unproven theorem, with no more sophisticated apparatus than pencil and paper, is a more radical aberration; yet it would seem capricious to deny him or her the title of researcher. But when one moves to consider the classicist or the academic teacher of literature, there is less tendency to describe his or her activities as the generation of knowledge, and a more natural inclination to see it as the creative reinterpretation of existing material.[10]

He suggests a continuum between research and scholarship which accomodates more academic teachers in various specialties and asks simply that they be "up-to-date and display an advanced mastery of their subject matter." At least the continuum suits reality.

The debate over research and teaching has long been in progress, but the nature and costs of the research have changed the arguments. Today, the questions are whether research is worth it, whether it merely gratifies the professor's egocentric interests, whether it is dangerous to human beings, and whether it is vital to teaching. In many countries the public is asking—with tax monies in mind—for better teaching with results that are self-evident in graduates and their employment. As governments set the lines for account- ability, the research–teaching allotment will be most pertinent, and on this point again academic autonomy is called into question.

9
CURRICULAR CHANGE
AND DIRECTIONS

Change is naturally a recurrent theme in any statement on what is happening in higher education systems around the world. Thus far, structural and organizational changes have been described—changes in governance, the location of power, the creation of new bodies or adjustments in the responsibilities of old ones, especially for planning, coordination, and management. Further changes affecting academic autonomy, admission policies, and research have also been discussed. In this chapter attention turns to curricular change, the organization of studies, teaching methods, and new "delivery systems."

Authors of the country reports were asked to comment on whether their higher education system is flexible and innovative, whether there are mechanisms to facilitate change, and where the initiative lies for curricular reforms. They were requested to given examples and explain how a particular change was accomplished or how and why it failed. In their answers, several authors lead with sentences on obstacles to change, and all the rest mention hindrances at one point or another in their statements. Our analysis follows their lead, and after discussing difficulties, we will consider the forces for change and directions in which changes are moving with regard to the curriculum, teaching, and students.

OBSTACLES

In describing higher education systems, the country reports use the words *resistance*, *constraints*, *obstacles*, *conservatism*, *tradition*, *preservation*, and *cultural heritage*. And the reference is more often to universities than to other sectors of higher education systems. Universities, as the established aristocrats and the relatively more autonomous units of the systems, seem to be able to fend off change and to endure in their customary basic practices more successfully than other types of higher education institutions.

Professors and Disciplines

The conservative nature of university professors is a worldwide phenomenon, though their influence varies with the historical development of the different countries' structures for higher education. Although they have not had the singular power in the United States and other English-speaking countries that they have enjoyed in the European model as seen in France and West Germany or as adapted in Japan, professors are still a force on the conservative side and frequently viewed as the main obstacle to change.

Jan Szczepański comments on the attitude of academic teachers:

Professors and other teachers have only on-the-job training in teaching. They have learned the methods of teaching by imitating their own professors, and I rather think that here is the main cause of the conservatism of higher education.

. . .

Although somewhat discredited by the mass increase in numbers of professors, the old tradition that a professor is the highest authority in his field of knowledge is still a force that obstructs innovations.[1]

From the United States, Lyman Glenny reflects agreement and suggests another reason: "Perhaps, as is the case for faculties in Europe and elsewhere, the amount of time and costs each faculty member has invested in his or her area of specialization makes it uncomfortable or unprofitable to change."[2]

In the last decades, professorial fiefdoms in France, West Germany, and Sweden have been converted into more departmental units of organization. Thus individual autocrats have joined together into oligarchic authorities,[3] but, throughout these adjustments, collegial rule has continued with its disciplinary base, just as it has held in the universities of other countries. Professorial authority, singly or collegially exercised, has proved itself to be a formidable stronghold of the status quo.

Sweden has seriously attempted reform by creating Researach and Development units at all universities for in-service training of teachers. The intent is to stimulate "critical thinking about education and its traditional forms" to help teachers innovate. However, the report cautions that the program for faculty development should not conceal the Swedish system's basic similarity with other countries' systems. The dominant features are:

...that activities are based on disciplines; that subject departments are the fundamental organizational units; and that the primary functions of the system are the production of new knowledge through research, the production of new producers of knowledge through postgraduate education, and the transmittal of knowledge through undergraduate education. These characteristics govern the system and the behavior within it more than anything else. And it is in such common determinants that we must seek the most important explanations of conditions and constraints for radical change.[4]

Before taking a totally negative view toward professorial attitudes and disciplinary allegiance, it must be noted that the obstacle in one set of circumstances can be a saving grace in another situation. Brian MacArthur emphasizes the staying power of the classroom and teacher regardless of government intervention and grand visions for change. The British report also credits the professor's natural satisfaction when the course goes well with many qualified students. Why change "at the behest of an educational television fanatic?"[5]

The Polish study registers similar points: first, that considerable autonomy endures in classroom teaching regardless of a communist-dominated political economy; and second, that change should not be of the radical, disruptive sort which disorganizes activities. The responsibility of educating the next generation for 40 years of professional activities requires that change be carefully prepared and slowly, but steadily implemented.[6] Clearly, change for its own sake is questionable.

The disciplinary base of educational organization has built its reward system on the foundations of research and publication, which are the "career currency" of professors. To expect them to commit themselves to change, for example, to interdisciplinary teaching is "to ask them to act as missionaries in a foreign land from which return home is difficult if not impossible."[7] Tony Becher's analogy from the British study concludes that although some teachers admirably make such attempts, it is not surprising that new institutions based on abandonment of traditional subject boundaries gradually revert to the discipline-based norm. The disciplinary lodestone holds a powerful attraction that specialization constantly renews.

Whatever the reasons for their position, teachers, especially at the higher ranks, tend to prefer the present way of doing things and seldom initiate change on a significant scale. Lyman Glenny ranks higher education's constituencies in terms of their conservative attitudes: "Much evidence supports the view that faculties adhere to the status quo more than administrators do, and administrators more than students."[8]

Administrators

Administrators, in their turn, are rewarded for the smooth functioning of the institution or the system. Seldom is one given a merit badge for rocking the boat and upsetting the system by doing something a different way, even though it might prove more effective than the established routine. There is little incentive for administrators personally to advocate innovative change.

Moreover, change is a lot of bother involving more problems and work in addition to what is already expected. Reassignment of personnel at any level is difficult and may require complicated negotiations with both individuals and bargaining agents. Approval for the contemplated change is needed from higher powers or democratic committees, depending on the system's structure. Usually both are necessary, and certainly a body of opinion must support the change if it is to move from paper and words into reality with any chance of survival.

Not only are salesmanship and conviction in the value of change required from the administrator, but generosity as well in giving the credit to others who join and help to bring the idea to fruition. Without attributing credit for the new program to those who carry it out, the program will surely wither away and die after its enthusiastic birth.

The qualities of leadership are far from innate in administrators. Yet, significant innovation cannot occur without leadership, or at least support, from the administration. Too often, followers are chosen for administrative appoinment rather than leaders. The follower is a known quantity to those participating in the selection process. To the faculty, he represents their views; to the board of trustees or directors, he presents no threat that he will upset the equilibrium; and to bureaucrats above in ministries, he understands the rules of the game and will see to it that things function smoothly.

Bureaucracy itself—stationed around or within administration—at the different levels in higher education systems is a force toward conformity and conservative routine which tends to restrict individual initiative and questioning of current procedures and programs. Civil servants representing governmental machinery are not apt to be encouraging either to institutional administrators who attempt innovation or to one of their own administrative staff who tries to improve bureaucratic practices.

Further, standardization of reporting techniques in efforts to get comparable data from various units of the system acts as a restraint on innovation or significant change in the way things are done. The insistence on comparative statistics from government offices, understandable for planning and funding purposes, can be counter-productive for educational change within the system. It only makes innovation harder if it involves different measurements of faculty and student time, for example, or different means of evaluating student achievement. Such changes are integral to basic experimentation in teaching and learning, but then translation must be devised to interpret the change in terms compatible with customary patterns.

Administrators inevitably must start with the inherited situation of their offices. Certain responsibilities are given them. And another set of limits exists in the length of their term of office. Frequently, it is not long enough to achieve much in the way of innovation or basic change.

In the European systems, traditionally, the administrative level has been relatively weak and professors took their turn in rotation as rector of the institution. There was more formality than substance in the position as decisive lines continued between influential professors and state officials. Recent reforms have strengthened the institutional presidency in France and lengthened the term of office to five years; West Germany too has increased the role of local administration; and the title of president is more prevalent in the European system.

Even though reforms are in this direction, the European type of system does not give administrators anything like the powers and responsibilities awarded to university presidents in the United States. Nor is there any expectancy that administrators should bring about miraculous change in the nationally centralized systems. Britain, for somewhat different reasons, does not ask its vice-chancellors to lead in the cause of change. And Japan is in a half-way position with the heads of national universities comparable to their European prototype and the heads of private sector institutions comparable to the United States pattern.

In none of the countries is the presidency or its equivalent office expected to provide leadership for change and innovation as in the United States. But here the factors are shifting too; presidents have less power than formerly, faculties and unionization are gaining strength, trustees are assuming more responsibilities, and students play a greater part. Presidents, also faced with financial problems whether in public or private institutions, are staying in office shorter terms and leaving less of a personal stamp on the institution's development. Small wonder that a survey of United States college and university presidents in 1975 indicated that only a small fraction of them anticipated much change in the next five years; most presidents projected "more extensions of what they had been doing" in the last five years since 1970.[9]

There are ample reasons for administrators to adhere to the status quo and not launch great reforms for improvement. They may be less conservative than professors whose first loyalty is to subject disciplines because they must see the whole institution and interpret it to the several publics asking questions. Often, however, administrators are unable, for many reasons, to lead real change. The conclusion might be drawn that administrators are lucky if they can keep an institution fairly flexible and receptive to new ideas.

Students

Glenny's evidence indicates that students are less wedded to the status quo than administrators. Undoubtedly true, but student attitudes show an ambivalence that is not easy to sort out or predict. As transients in the educational process, they do not represent steady, consistent positions on academic issues. Not infrequently, they are conservative toward their own education, as it concerns themselves, while they advocate major changes on broader issues—political, economic, and social.

On other occasions, students have stood for radical change, both in governance and curricula, within higher education systems. In contrast with the era of the late 1960s and early 1970s, students today are generally more withdrawn, concentrating on academic matters, and competing intensely for advancement toward tighter job markets. They are currently in a rather conservative stance.

Students do not flock to experimental colleges in the United States; the majority seeks established institutions with known reputations and standard courses of study. Many fear changes in grading systems and evaluation that may not be easily understood by graduate and professional schools they wish to enter. Their fear is understandable in light of graduate program routines. Little change occurs there to encourage undergraduate innovation. Graduate level studies provide the capstone of reward for conservative preparation in the traditional mold.

A case in point is the French student reaction in the spring of 1976 when reform was ordered for the *maîtrise*, the second cycle. Universities were "to reorganize their studies, to combine old courses differently, and to create new courses more relevant to the wide range of available nonacademic opportunities." The new degrees for the second cycle were to have the status of national degrees after approval of the then Secretary of State for Universities upon recommendation of professionals and professors.

The reform had been proposed because many students, especially in literary and scientific programs designed to train secondary school teachers, could not expect employment in these traditional fields. Unfortunately, the reform was handicapped by no allotment of funds for the change and complicated by the opposition of teachers whose courses would have to be changed or eliminated. So the new programs were branded "narrowly professional" and the reform a "business takeover" of the universities. A reform with reasonable objectives, developed over two years with care and consultations, met unexpected hostility from the combined force of teachers and students.

> The student body felt that preprofessional programs accomplish little with respect to the unemployment problem and, actually, lead to dead ends. The students, coming increasingly from the middle classes, can expect to obtain only middle-management jobs with their single university diploma. From the students' perspective, the university would propose 'too much work' for limited opportunities and little chance of advancement.[10]

The students wanted, at least, a choice. Strikes were extensive, lasting more than two months, and 60 thousand students took late examinations.

The Secretary of State for Universities compromised the reform effort and offered universities the possiblity of retaining "existing fundamental programs."

The French example had political and economic forces involved that influenced student attitudes. In other cases students have actively promoted curricular reforms as they did in the late 1960s in the United States. At that time they pressed for more "relevance" in courses, less rigid requirements, and multidisciplinary studies. They had a pronounced effect, and many institutions changed in those directions. Students can constitute an overwhelming force in sheer numbers and, as the direct expression of market demand, they can be as effective on the part of conservative interests as on more radical issues.

Funds

One of the errors apparent in the French reform was the lack of funds to help bring about the needed changes. Few countries have made allocations in any significant amount to support educational research, experimental attempts, or major changes, even when they have been legislated.

Unlike scientific research and changes in medical education or other scientific fields, research and change in the social sciences and humanities are expected without an additional financial commitment of any size. In fact, support monies diminish steadily in the order in which the fields are mentioned. Therefore, as might be expected, government funds are not readily awarded to further improvements generally in higher education systems. Governments have a record of supporting the building of new institutions and the purchase of new equipment—hardware—but little record for significant changes in the academic programs of established institutions.

In France, the problem is particularly severe. The total operating budget of universities not only failed to keep pace with inflation (true in other countries as well), but the 5 percent of operating funds that, in the past, were reserved "theoretically" for innovation has been cut off.[11] The United States higher education system is not quite so badly off, as yet. It is likely, however, as cutbacks increase with rising costs and falling enrollments, that funds for innovation will be among the first to go.

At present, some states offer funds "for competition among the institutions in developing innovations in program, delivery systems, or in the organization of curricula."[12] While the funds are not large, institutional competition has produced significant programs along the lines intended by the states. Federal funds are available through several agencies, and private foundations make grants for innovative programs, but their assets are reduced, grants tend to be smaller, and high risk or real venture funds are not easily to be found.

Both federal and foundation awards are for fairly short time periods—intended to launch but not maintain a new project. So, unless the state or the institution can continue the program in the future, the application may be ill-advised. Moreover, both federal and foundation grants are being made increasingly on a matching basis, with the institution to raise a matching amount, in order to stimulate initiative and stretch the dollar amount. Although the United States is clearly better off than many countries funding toward change, it is not a happy picture.

Sweden, on the other hand, has taken responsibility for experimentation and major change in its higher education system. The concept of experimentation is implemented through the institutional research and development units, and education committees that are charged with curricular improvement. The Swedish report, therefore, does not complain about the lack of funds for innovation; constraints, however, exist, and the report points out that although money and organization are there, the results are generally disappointing.

The Iranian report also registers no complaint about lack of funds as a reason for the general failure of attempts to innovate. Instead, one of their main problems has been instability of political support since there have been five different ministers in charge of policy making for higher education during the last ten years. As the report wisely states: "Generous allocation of financial resources, alone, cannot really change the direction of universities."[13] The conditions for change and creative innovation go well beyond funding, but the absence of financial incentive and means can be a serious handicap.

FORCES FOR CHANGE

In view of the formidable odds against it, change, in any meaningful amount, is the more remarkable. Still, the forces motivating change can be very strong. Usually located *outside* the higher education system, they are external forces propelled by political pressures, economic needs, and people's demands. External forces may be joined, rapidly or slowly, by individuals and groups internal to the system. Or, if the forces are resisted and the system appears recalcitrant, the chances are that alternative structures will be created to accomplish the desired purpose.

Political Pressures

The biggest change in the last quarter of a century—the move to mass education—was stimulated by three external pressures in unison. Political forces, in the form of government, seized the initiative and financially supported the move; people grasped the opportunity, producing mass enrollment; and the economic needs of growth sustained the purpose and provided the outlet for graduate employment.

The increase in enrollment brought with it political pressures that democratized the internal governance of higher education systems and their institutions. Broader participation of the various constituencies has changed the forums in which policies and decisions are made. Participatory democracy in the United States system has reached the unruly point, in some cases, of constituencies' questioning the right of their elected representatives to speak for them; the issue must return for referendum to all members of the group. This delays and cripples action, and strengthens self-interest groups at the expense of the majority. The limits of participatory democracy are being tested.

Besides student representation, junior faculty (assistant level and lecturers) have gained admittance and a voice, often with vote, in deliberations formerly restricted to top-level professors. The younger academic ranks frequently advance more liberal positions on issues than professors and push for more radical reforms on both educational and political matters. On occasion, they are very responsive to external political pressures advocating radical change, and they form a first line of support for such change within universities.

Party lines of the left—socialist and communist oriented—have, in some countries, connected directly with campuses through younger faculty as well as students. France and West Germany, in particular have witnessed such action on university campuses that constitute voting blocks of importance in general elections. Within some universities, "red islands" championing communist doctrine have appeared in academic programs. They challenge the claim of objectivity in teaching and whether the disinterested search for truth is not a camouflage for accepted capitalist doctrine.

Whatever the cause supported, higher education systems are being drawn more and more into political affairs in many countries; and higher education policies are an important element in party platforms. An example mentioned earlier is the creation of regional boards in Sweden which are a consequence of political party compromise. The Swedish report especially draws attention to the politicization that is happening in the higher education system as corporate, labor, community, and political interests are more extensively represented.

European universites, on the whole, are close and more integrally related to political activities than those in the English-speaking countries. The British, Canadian, American, and Australian systems have lagged compared to other countries of the world. Thailand, Iran, Mexico, and Latin America, on the other hand, are accustomed to university involvement with revolution. From the foundation upward, the structure and functioning of

higher education has broadened horizontally in numbers of people participating and interests represented. Signs indicate that political pressures will be
seen and felt increasingly in campus affairs.

Economic Needs

Economic progress and manpower needs are dominant among national
goals for higher education. In this regard, political interests and economic
forces have joined hands in a powerful union to further the goal. Together,
they constitute strong leverage for change in higher education systems. There
was ample evidence in the review of goals showing the adjustments that have
been made or are in the process as a result of society's economic
requirements.

Australia's report traces clearly the influence of manpower needs in the
evolution of its system of higher education. During the late 1950s, the
Murray Committee on Australian Universities maintained that the most
urgent demand on universities was for the provision of graduates:

> Industry and commerce call for more graduates, government and public
> administration call for more graduates, and all the services of the welfare
> state call for more graduates...every boy or girl with the necessary
> brainpower must, in the national interest, be encouraged to come forward
> for a university education.[14]

Later, the Martin Committee continued the emphasis on the provision of
manpower. And Bruce Williams says that it was because the government
accepted this line of thought that it provided funds for the great increase in
university education, in teachers' colleges and then colleges for advanced
education, and now for the current drive to expand technical and further
education. Perceived economic needs, endorsed and financially underwritten
by government have directly shaped the system.

In a more sporadic way, the Japanese system showed its direct response
to external economic need when business and corporate groups pressured for
a rapid increase in scientific and technological training and they got it—a
remarkable number of graduates from these fields in a few years. Every
country provides many examples that attest to the dominance of economic
demand and the changes that have happened as a result.

Economic factors have influenced the structure of Sweden's system,
reshaping the actual organization into divisions that parallel the job market
for graduates. The National Board of Universities and Colleges has been
reorganized so that five planning commissions correspond to large sectors of
the labor market:

Technical Professions & Natural and Technical Sciences
Administrative, Economic, and Social Professions & Social Science and Law
Medical and Nursing Professions & Medicine, Odontology, and Pharmacy
Teaching Professions
Cultural and Information Professions & Humanities and Theology[15]

Education and research bureaus, which connect these five commissions to the institutions in the system, translate the professional needs for the traditional faculty areas. In addition, the new regional boards are seen as replicas of the national board's organization; they too are to plan according to the same labor market sectors.

Such organized planning exists in few countries. Most of the systems are out of kilter with the job market, and the majority are leaving the adjustment generally to the marketplace. The United States, Canada, and the United Kingdom count mainly on the flexibility of the market, and, to some extent, the more general training and adjustability of their graduates. Specialization and narrow professionalism are not typical in these countries for students with the B.A. degree; liberal arts is the pattern.

West Germany, in contrast, has operated with a lock-step between its higher education and employment systems that now poses a tremendous problem. The German authors call it another bottleneck, the first being the large number of students qualified for entry to the higher education system. In effect, the system is blocked at both entrance and exit points by the numbers of students.

For years, the civil service has been the primary employer of graduates, accepting in recent years two-thirds of all graduates from higher education. A high degree of professionalism characterized their studies, which were also adjusted in length to fit categories legally set in the ranks of the civil service system. Today there are simply too many graduates to accomodate, and society's needs have shifted, for example, in numbers of teachers required for elementary and secondary schools. Major adjustments are needed in the higher education systems which, some have judged, would be easier to change than the career system so deeply embedded in "paper qualifications" and society's perspectives.[16] No other country in our study has such frustration and seemingly insurmountable problems. France shares them, but to a lesser degree.

Nevertheless, the overproduction of graduates in most developed countries, the crowning success of the movement to mass enrollment, has meant defeat for considerable numbers of graduates in job placement. Overproduction in certain fields has led to limited opportunities and employment that is inadequate to their training. In this dilemma, the free market wastes talents. And the situation is futher aggravated in some countries by general unemployment rates. Many factors cannot be controlled, short of a planned economy in an authoritarian setting, and even then more wisdom and foresight is called for than man usually has demonstrated.

Higher education systems seldom march to the fluctuating rhythms of the marketplace, much less keep pace with manpower projections that have too often failed to call the tune. But they do follow along, shifting and changing as they go. There is no question about the force of economic needs as a factor in higher education; it is simply that systems are generally slow in their response.

When, however, the economy as a whole suffers a setback and financial exigency takes over, higher education systems, like other social institutions, immediately feel the impact. Adjustments are prompted to speed up and changes occur more quickly. After the usual procedures of percentage cuts in all areas and deferral of some items, systems and individual institutions are forced to reassess priorities and ways of doing the job. It is in this stage that constructive efforts can be made and quality improved, in the face of necessity. Financial cutbacks mean inevitable decline in quality only when it is assumed that all was fine and of high quality with a full budget. Necessity has more than once fostered imagination and invention, and brought forth the best of human resources. In the immediate period ahead, for most of the countries, economic factors undoubtedly will be the greatest of the forces for change in higher education systems.

Student Demand

Student demand gets its force from numbers—mass backing. We have commented on the far-reaching effects of massive growth creating the systems approach, on the changes brought to student bodies in composition and a growing age divergence. Student movements en masse have effected basic and long-lasting reforms in governing procedures, and, in European countries especially, students are a force in framing political policy.

At this point, we turn to student force in changing curricular patterns. It has been said students register with their feet—where they go in course selection has a great influence on the curriculum. Their shifts and changes in course enrollments create imbalance in departmental staffing and in the use of facilities. More liberal study regulations—fewer required courses and prerequisites for sequential learning—allow more flexibility and student shifts can be greater and more extreme. In the United States, where required course patterns were relaxed in response to student demand in the late sixties, the problem of enrollment shifts has been most acute. West Germany, at the other extreme, holding highly structured requirements, has no doubt seen fewer shifts in student enrollment patterns. Choices are more prescribed.

In their initial choice of field or major for study, however, students in systems everywhere reflect the major currents in society. Thus, in the overall picture, we see large numbers choosing law, growing numbers entering the world of computers, steady demand for medicine—the most competitive of professional fields in all the countries—and shifts in engineering, technical, and managerial areas. Higher education institutions perforce must change and, occasionally, the change is innovative.

The British report makes the strongest statement for the influence of student enrollment demands on innovation. Hampered by stereotypes, one does not somehow expect the British to express forcefully the crass reality of the student marketplace; that role belongs to the pragmatic American. But then, one did not expect the bold creation of the Open University on British shores either.

Tony Becher's argument for the power of student demand runs thus:

> The healthy maintenance of any institution of higher education—and indeed of any individual sub-group such as a department or school of study—depends on its ability to attract students in numbers sufficient to justify its current levels of staffing and other resources. Since the world outside changes itself with very little regard to the convenience and comfort of academics, this often means that, whether the staff concerned like it or not, they may have to introduce substantial (and sometimes major) innovations simply in order to remain in business.[17]

The example chosen is classics, for many years a most prestigious subject and considered the proper preparation of statesmen to guide the country. Its old preeminence has declined rapidly for a whole host of reasons including "an increasingly utilitarian emphasis in social institutions, and a strong political reaction against elitism in education." Classicists, for reasons outside thier control, "have had little choice between innovation and immolation."

Chemistry departments, too, have actively mobilized their inventive resources, and Becher expresses the belief that teachers in a given subject area can rapidly and extensively respond in anticipation of a threat to student recruitment. Some have survived by initiative in making basic curricular changes and even through novelty in pedagogic style. Student demand—an additional force from the marketplace—has gained power in the last decade and, along with political policies and economic factors, has become a major reason for program innovation.

PROCESSES

As pressures mount from the various sources, and depending on their nature, they can take formation as national legislation that causes the most sweeping changes, generally affecting all parts of higher education systems. Such is the case with national reforms enacted in France, Sweden, and West Germany—countries where legislated changes have been fairly specific and extensive. Comparative analyses of systems are too apt, however, to expect nationally legislated reforms primarily in centralized nations, so it is well to notice the inclusion of the Federal Republic of Germany in this approach.

Furthermore, both policy and funding changes on the part of federal as well as unitary governments can basically alter higher education systems without ever being called a "reform." For example, marked change and innovation came with the growth of mass education which, in many countries was simply accomplished by extending educational benefits gradually to more and more people, changing entrance standards, increasing student aid, and providing additional facilities. They were radical changes in the potential implications, yet they were not heralded as national reforms.

In other cases, such national actions have been incorporated in more comprehensive legislation covering many aspects of higher education systems, often with detailed changes, and sometimes stating a new emphasis or goal. While statements of this sort are more likely to appear from centralized governments exercising their sole responsibility for higher education, they may also come from federal governments with caveats of due regard for state or provincial responsiblity.

Other types of reform and change may, of course, occur only on the state–provincial level in the federal organization, but have equally significant impact on the higher education system within its jurisdiction. On either governmental level, the processes followed may be similar, so the discussion does not separate the levels.

Ad Hoc Commissions

Some countries effectively use ad hoc commissions to study issues, collect information, and prepare recommendations for governmental action. It is customary to have academic representatives on the commissions for the expertise and knowledge they can bring to the issue, and for their value in serving as interpreters of the recommendations—a bridge—back to the educational community. Moreover, the final legislation may not be so far off target or so inappropriate for higher education systems as it might be without the educators' participation in the process.

In the United Kingdom, Australia, Canada, and Sweden especially, ad hoc commissions are customarily the first step toward innovation on a wide scale. Edward Sheffield claims that in Canada, in the past 25 years, the major changes in systems of higher education can be traced to just such bodies.[18] Britain had the famous Robbins' Committee; Australia the Murray, Martin, and Kangan committees; and Sweden's central government draws extensively on ad hoc committees, not only for national reforms, but also in the regular functioning of the Office of the Chancellor of the National Board for Universities and Colleges. Such commissions appear to operate most successfully as part of the general consultative practice that is integral to the Swedish system. Although ad hoc commission reports have not always recommended the changes finally adopted in these countries, they have generally led the significant moves for change, and thus guided development of the higher education systems.

Japan first established an ad hoc committee in the early 1970s. It was the Study Committee on Higher Education referred to earlier on planning, which was its function. With the publishing of its final report in 1976, the committee's work ended, but its subcommittee for planning was attached to the University Chartering Board and continues to act as the official consultative organ to the Ministry of Education. The proposals for comprehensive planning issued as the final report are expected to play a large role in administrative decision making and so affect change in the system.[19]

An ad hoc planning committee in Thailand proposed the establishment of the University Development Commission which the Cabinet approved in 1967. For the ten years of its existence, the commission of university educators and related government officials worked to improve the quality of graduate programs and training of university teachers. Its function was eventually absorbed by the Office of University Affairs.[20]

The United States has not used ad hoc commissions as effectively as these other countries. Presidents have appointed comparable groups on higher education, often called "task forces," but recommendations have seldom been heeded. It is possible that directives were too broad, lacking specificity, and that membership was too limited in that educators mainly comprised the committees. Also, there is neither tradition to support the attention of Congress and government offices to proposals so made, nor machinery to link them to the ongoing process. As a result, task forces have come and gone on many issues, leaving it to chance if their recommendations are acted upon.

Privately established commissions have had more impact than those under government sponsorship. During the last decade or so, the Carnegie Commission, and the Council for Policy Studies in Higher Education, both under Clark Kerr's leadership, have been the most effective voice nationally on major issues. The Council has now ceased to exist, and it remains to be seen if private initiative will soon provide again such leadership. The experiences of ad hoc committees in the other English-speaking countries and Sweden, where they have long records, could profitably be studied by the United States and other nations.

After the initial stage, where ad hoc commissions may be most instrumental in framing the concept and directions for change, there comes the time for deliberate decision concerning the means to be employed. Assuming favorable reaction in whole or part to the commission's recommendations, government may legislate, if necessary, or change policies where possible to effect the reform. It may fund experimentation to test out possibilities as several governments are doing and, under certain conditions, government may choose to create alternative institutions and new forms of higher education. Most have taken this route to supplement or circumvent the university establishment. In addition, from the institutional viewpoint, there is always incremental change, not necessarily involving deliberate choice, that goes on continually. Each of these three types of approaches is discussed.

Experimentation

The best way to try out an innovation before a large scale adoption that could be disastrous is to experiment with it—to launch a pilot project. It does not require great outlays of funds, and it encourages initiative on the part of applicants in a competitive situation. Further, there is the chance if it succeeds that others will adopt the model.

The United States and West Germany are using this approach more than the other nations, but no doubt for very different reasons. The experimental idea appeals to the American temperament: initiative, competition, and not too much money at the beginning. The Germans, more than likely, appreciate the experimental method because it involves research and is cautious—before a wholesale application. Although both countries are trying the pilot approach, neither shows significant results. It may be too early in the West German case, but the United States has long favored experiments even though they have seldom served their model purpose. Lyman Glenny wisely observes that perhaps the experiments are not well chosen. Depending on the process of approval for experimental programs and who is deciding, "quite possibly the most prosaic of them" get the stamp of approval.[21] Judges are not always given to an experimental outlook.

Federal support for curricular experimentation is fairly extensive, coming from various government agencies, though not great in dollar amounts. The relatively new Fund for Innovation in Postsecondary Education has established a good record in backing unusual and interesting types of programs; the National Science Foundation has encouraged curricular projects in sciences, and the National Endowments for the Arts and Humanities have broadened support in the creative and liberal arts. Private foundations traditionally provide an important source for experimental programs but, in recent years, they have taken less risks and supplied less capital.

Compared to other countries, the United States record may appear enviable, but little has happened as a result of many curricular experiments. Factual evidence does not indicate that models are often copied or adjusted elsewhere. Follow-up and objective analysis of flaws are lacking and, too frequently, the recipient of project funds claims general achievement. Curricular experimentation, however, is not without other advantages: it furnishes leverage toward change within an institution or on a small scale, and reforms that may last in that setting. And it is particularly valuable insofar as faculty members take the initiative and carry out the project.

In the last decade, West Germany's Federal-State Commission has inaugurated a program of pilot projects which is considered an important addition to diverse attempts at study reform. Started in 1971, there were 90 government subsidized experiments six years later. The program is much more structured and tightly organized than comparable efforts in the United States:

> The working group, Pilot Projects in Higher Education, is responsible for the coordination of pilot projects. It is a subgroup of the Committee for Innovations in the Educational System of the Federal-State Commission (BLK). Like the composition of the BLK, it is staffed with representatives of the ministries of culture—eleven delegates of the Länder and two Bund representatives—but no university representatives. Those who are interested in carrying out pilot projects can only submit their suggestions to the respective Ministry of Culture, which will then decide whether to use this suggestion for its own proposal to the BLK. This means that the cultural government agencies have virtually complete control over this reform instrument.[22]

Besides clearance at both state and national levels, innovative projects must conform to the objectives and planning of Bund and Länder, be designed to facilitate decisions that concern the development of the system, and produce results that would be applicable to other areas in higher education—not just other institutions. Further, a regionally balanced distribution of projects with comparable subjects and quality is desired, and they are to be implemented cooperatively by government and institutions of higher education. They are also subject to systematic reporting and evaluation.

Just over half of the 13 concentrations for pilot projects deal with university and study reforms, and a sizeable number of projects are operative in one concentration. For example, 11 projects are to increase efficiency of teaching and learning by using media (including measures to shorten the length of studies and residence). Nine are to develop graduated programs of study represented in universities and in *Fachhochschulen*, such as integrated programs for architecture and technology.

The evaluation of projects toward improvement in a certain problem area is greatly facilitated by having several comparable projects underway at one time and distributed regionally over the country. Once again, nations could well study practices elsewhere to their own enlightenment and possible benefit. In the case of experimental pilot programs, the West German experience could be instructive.

Alternative Institutions

By all odds, the most commonly used process to effect innovation is to bypass the establishment and set up new institutions for different purposes. It is simpler than struggling against the obstacles, accustomed ways are not disrupted, and fewer personnel are disturbed. Moreover, traditional institutions that are serving well need protection to carry on their programs. So the motives may be negative or affirmative in choosing the alternate route.

The bypass process is familiar and frequent as a pattern of growth in social institutions. Often additions constitute the solution to problems. The strategy is the same when an agency fails to carry out its responsibility or is unable to adjust for any reason; the answer is to create another agency or board for the needed function rather than ask the existing one to change.

Thus, when universities in particular did not or could not accommodate the changing enrollment demands, additional places were created outside university walls. Sometimes the move involved a deliberate decision to save the university and its purposes from being overrun by the numbers of students desiring admission. Such was the thought, for example, in designing the three-sector structure for California:[23] the University of California and its branches, the state colleges, and the community colleges, with their many campuses. Each sector has expanded in its own way, but not without considerable friction, especially between the university and state colleges. On a country-wide basis, the United States has tended to add new types of institutions rather than count on existing ones to change drastically. Similar developments have taken place in many higher education systems as educational gaps were filled with new training opportunities.

One benefit is obvious from the bypass process: alternative institutions and programs immediately increase diversity in educational forms, which is of utmost importance if systems are to meet the various needs and interests of people in further learning. However, while choice is widening for people, and greater numbers of students are being accommodated, the balance of numbers within higher education systems is shifting in a pronounced way. Changes are happening more *around* universities than *within* them. Growing numbers of students in comprehensive colleges and shorter-term programs for vocational–technical training gradually change the percentages toward the newer programs.

In other words, the proportion of all students in newer, alternative programs is growing steadily as the numbers enrolled in universities remain relatively static or begin to decline (the birthrate factor) in most developed countries. The lower birthrate may be expected to reduce university enrollments more than alternative institutions that welcome adults and offer more courses oriented to career interest and contemporary concerns.

Most important, political interests and financing formulas tend to favor increasing numbers—where the large numbers of students are. So it is no surprise to find many governments increasing their support particularly for technical and vocational programs and adult enrollment. This can produce difficulties in maintaining first-class universities; public support cannot be taken for granted to the extent it was in the past. Competition, born of enrollment growth in alternative programs, has increased markedly for the university sector in higher education systems.

Sweden has not created alternative institutions to any significant extent. The single pattern in Sweden has been "to build new universities as miniature copies of the old ones." To be sure, there was a slight deviation in 1967 when "university branches" were started in four medium-sized cities with the express intent to concentrate on undergraduate education (no postgraduate or research function). But, each branch was under the authority of a university and, by 1976, the one at Linköping had gained the status of an independent university. No alternative purpose was really intended.

Bertil Östergren explains that the Swedish system with its central regulation and network of legal rules has hampered local initiatives for radical change. Uniformity is the striking feature of the system, which makes it "more resistant to system-deviating innovations," but which, at the same time, "facilitates national reforms."[24] By legislated edict, Sweden has undertaken major national reforms to decentralize, to open up opportunities for adults, to stress undergraduate teaching, and career-orientation in studies— highly significant changes. The method chosen, however, was not creating a really new sector of some sort, but asking the existing establishment to change.

Poland, another highly centralized nation, indicates no significant adoption or creation of alternative types of institutions in its higher education system. Nor has France made startling innovations. The University Institutes of Technology are the primary new addition; the reorganization into units of instruction and research (UERs) as subdivisions of universities is basically a structural reform within the establishment. Neither Iran nor Mexico has inaugurated alternative institutions on any scale. Of the countries in the study, most of those with more centralized and uniform higher education systems have not chosen to expand opportunities by building extensive alternate facilities. Instead they have tried reforms, usually national in scope, to change the established system.

Thailand and Japan are exceptional in creating private colleges as alternative forms of higher education: Thailand, for its ten colleges of business and commerce set up since 1969, and Japan, for its extensive creation of junior colleges and private universities under United States influence since World War II. Neither, however, has directly affected the older traditional university system.

Meanwhile, several other countries have started new types of institutions, sometimes *de novo* and, in other instances, by combining and changing existing institutions to fill apparent needs. Two- and three-year institutions generally are new creations, while four-year types have more often resulted from amalgamation and upgrading of colleges of education, of commerical and technical institutes, and sometimes small professional schools. The four-year programs are naturally closer to alternatives for universities, since they offer undergraduate work at roughly comparable level.

Britain's 30 polytechnic institutions and Australia's Colleges of Advanced Education are illustrative; compared to universities, they are more comprehensive in concept, including vocational purposes, and they offer subdegree as well as degree work. In their governance, they are closer to their communities or local state authorities than the more autonomous universities, and they are expected to respond to the needs of their areas by offering suitable curricular programs. Flexibility is more inherent, and change is, therefore, simpler to accomplish. Four-year institutions of this sort commonly form a sector in the higher education system that is distinct and separate from the universities.

Mergers of smaller or outmoded institutions have also produced new units for university sectors as they have enlarged with enrollment, but these have been fashioned on the university model. Although they have become alternative *institutions*, they have not provided alternative *forms* of higher education. Hence, they are not innovative; they merely offer additional places in the already accepted pattern. Many universities in the United States followed this route, creating branch campuses and multi-campus systems on the state level. And most countries, to a greater or lesser degree, have so expanded the number of universities.

The shorter-term programs of community and junior colleges, one- to three-year technical schools, and further training aimed at vocational preparation have had the greatest growth and are the major innovation, particularly in Canada, Australia, and the United States. These types are by far the most flexible and serviceable in response to area needs, and they have contributed greatly in the geographic distribution of learning. Student bodies typically range from upper-secondary years through adult ages and, depending on the institutional purposes, may be engaged either in practical courses of a vocational, terminal nature or in general studies equivalent to the first two years of college for transfer into a higher institution.

Canada is developing a wide array of such short-term institutions, especially in the Western provinces where the form has rapidly caught hold. British Columbia, Alberta, and Saskatchewan have each started community colleges on distinctive lines. In some cases, former technical or vocational schools have merged to form community colleges.

Saskatchewan is most innovative and unique in its "middle range education" that operates without permanent facilities in 14 community districts. Carrying on the tradition of the University of Saskatchewan's strong extension service, founded under its first president in the early part of this century, community colleges serve adult students through decentralized services. The new system:

> ...emphasizes learning arrangements, rather than a physical plant; the structure is concerned more with its relation to other agencies than with the colleges as an institution per se.... An educational communications network (video, audio, film, print) is being incorporated within the college system to permit maximal accessibility to learning programs in a province with a substantial rural population.[25]

The community college sector contracts with existing technical institutes and the two universities, as well as the provincial library and government agencies for courses. The managing staff is small and so is the investment in capital resources; in practice, it is primarily a brokerage function that yields very high returns. In 1976, the third year of operation, there were 73,000 registrations in 5,500 college classes in 582 centers, an astounding record of growth.

Ontario and Quebec have also successfully inaugurated middle-range institutions, but of a more formal sort. In 1965, in response to the dramatic increases in enrollment, Ontario's creation of colleges for applied arts and technology (CAATs) was a "sudden and bold maneuver." Today, there are 22 CAATs, some with a number of campuses. Focus is on courses beyond the secondary level, though graduation is not required, and they have a broad mandate: to meet educational needs of adults and out-of-school youth, short of serving those who wish to attend a university. Residence is not necessarily intended; hence the designation "community colleges."

Quebec took a different track and integrated middle-range institutions into a continuum from primary and secondary schools to universities or employment. For all students there, the choice is to attend a College of General and Vocational Education (CEGEPs) for a two-year preparation for university education or three-year training for a job. Most important, there is no other regular route to the university. Further, the three-year vocational program is not absolutely terminal; if graduates have the prerequisites, they can enter universities and, under certain circumstances, the *Ecole de Technologie Supérieure* recently created at the *Université du Québec.* Established since 1967, there are now 37 CEGEPs that constitute "one of the more visible achievements of the 'Quiet Revolution' in Quebec."[26]

The creation and expansion of shorter-term programs for vocational and general purposes are probably the foremost curricular innovation in higher education systems in the last two decades. They provide not only alternative *routes* to the universities and higher colleges, but also alternative *forms* of education. The pattern holds great promise for the future, especially in its flexibility for change in course offerings, and its basic concept of service, through education, for young and older adults alike. Of the various innovations launched, the community college pattern presents the greatest possibilities for developing countries. Moreover, it invites adjustment to the country's own needs, its current situation, and historical context.

In awarding high honors to the community college movement as a foremost innovation in higher education systems a slight technical qualification is necessary. Since many of these institutions grew from public secondary school support, sponsored by local school boards and education agencies, they cannot be attributed to higher education's initiative. Only recently have community colleges and vocational-technical institutes of the middle range been incorporated into definitions of *higher* education and systems that include universities. In a sense, the greatest innovation was *given* to higher education systems from the outside.

Incremental Change

Less dramatic and rapid in expansion, less deliberately planned at inception, some changes slowly and constantly accumulate until they attract considerable attention and are labelled a "trend." Incremental change includes the type that Szczepański endorses as the "mechanism of self-adjustment" which is steady and continuous, not given to big reforms that disorganize activities. Research and evaluation are important components in the process if the change is really to effect improvement. In these components, the Polish system is reather weak and, for that matter, so are all the other systems in the study, even the Swedish system with built-in research and development units.

Although the essential research role is commonly unfilled, changes of this type are going on all the time, usually in an unplanned and uncoordinated manner; and they account, in large part, for basic curricular reforms that live on in accepted practice. Lyman Glenny observes that:

> Routine change, over time, causes accretionary but drastic revisions in the roles of institutions and the programs which they offer. This incremental and largely unplanned approach has created the main revisions in courses, programs, and delivery methods.[27]

When the reform comes from teachers, it is at the foundation of the system—teaching, content, and learning. To the degree that internal generation and individual initiative perform the act of change, the process will be congenial to professors and teachers. Compared, for example, to nationally enacted reforms for curricular matters which can easily go awry and fail in the teaching program, the more organic process of accretionary change has proved its effectiveness. Its formation rests on those responsible for carrying it out.

The crucial question today is whether the slower but effective process of incremental change can cope with many large-scale demands being made on higher education systems. Time is not necessarily on the systems' side to allow the cumulative approach, even though it is basic to the education students receive. An additional question has to be asked as well: how strongly motivated are faculty in taking the initiative for basic curricular reforms? The answer is discouraging. Reports do not reveal that faculty have instigated such changes in any sizeable way. Instead, reforms are generally motivated by elements entering from outside the classroom like student enrollment shifts and financial exigency, or political changes from a higher level in the system.

Incremental change happens, of course, in all aspects of higher education systems—for good or bad. Academic drift is illustrative of such change. Directives on any matter, aimed somewhat differently each year, produce gradual changes that can finally add up to major policy shifts. The budgetary process, allocating more in one area than another for expenditure, causes at the least an incremental change in the balance within an institution or among the sectors of a system. On the other hand, the common practice of incremental budget increases across the board does not make for adjustments; to the contrary, it can inhibit change and encourage maintainace of the status quo. And it leads to the usual pattern of expectancy that "business" will go on in the customary ways.

When the sources capable of causing small changes are recognized, along with their potential for amassing to the point of causing significant change, it is strange indeed to consider higher education in a "steady state" simply because great expansion and growth have ended in most developed countries. The phrase is misleading and even dangerous in the complacent assumption that all will continue as at present. External forces of change within society will never allow stasis to happen in human affairs, much less higher education.

DIRECTIONS

Regardless of differing approaches and circumstances in the countries, certain trends appear repeatedly in curricular discussions. They give promise of enduring and basically changing the curricula for higher education systems in the years ahead. The directions favored are:

1. The importance of teaching
2. Practical experience and career-orientation
3. Multidisciplinary approaches
4. Reduced study periods
5. New communication media

First, there is renewed attention and emphasis on teaching undergraduates, especially in four-year colleges and universities. The pendulum swinging between research and teaching currently rests on the latter. Problems of combining the two functions in universities are more openly recognized as in the British, Swedish, and Japanese references cited earlier.

Most of the new higher education institutions founded in the 12 countries are for teaching purposes; Sweden's new universities are specifically for undergraduate instruction, and the United States liberal arts programs in both public and private sectors are devoted primarily to teaching. Shorter-term programs, where the greatest expansion has occurred in most countries, are aimed exclusively at teaching.

Student evaluation has revealed shortcoming in teaching and raised consciousness about inadequacies in some United States institutions. At Yale and Columbia Universities, for example, students publish their evaluation of courses. While only a few institutions formally take student judgement into account when considering a teacher's promotion or renewal of contract, there is pressure from students to do so. Other countries' higher education systems would no doubt view this development with alarm. Nonetheless, it has heightened attention on teaching ability.

In one way or another, each report registers concern about the quality of teaching and the need for improvement. Faculty development is a topic on the United States agenda; we noted Mexico's problem with so many faculty teaching only part time, and Iran's lack of qualified professionals and dependence on foreign faculty. Thailand has tried special graduate training for students intending to become university teachers, but without success.

Sweden's in-service training for teachers and department chairmen (and other staff) is the most organized and extensive. Courses range in length from part of a day to several weeks, and attendance is voluntary. The weakness, at present, is that mainly committed, younger university lecturers are attracted, not the established professoriate. Believing in its potential for improvement, Sweden plans to enlarge the program so that all teachers will regularly attend a course.

Refresher or retraining courses for faculty are particularly important when we look ahead at changes that can be expected. New knowledge, with implications for all fields, is coming at a faster rate and requires constant study and course adjustments. Further, since the majority of faculty are either tenured or hold status as civil servants, many systems find themselves with a large proportion of faculty built in for some years to come and fewer opportunities to make new, younger appointments as enrollments decline and expansion ceases. Under the circumstances, retraining and development programs for faculty are essential. Higher education systems are well aware of the need and the problems, but none offers a solution.

The second direction for curricular change recognizes the value of practical experience in learning. It is reminiscent of Alfred North Whitehead's belief in forging the links between theory and concrete reality. The idea is not new to education generally, but it is new and growing in higher education circles. Theory finds it has a companion insisting on useful application.

For a long time, practice and work experience have been integral to vocational and technical schools. Practical work was essential for training in skills, and achievement was measured largely by performance criteria. Governments easily saw the immediate value of such skills in society and willingly put greater amounts of public funds into this type of training. The tremendous expansion of shorter-term programs—institutes, community colleges, middle-range institutions—has been the result. Apprenticeships are returning to favor, after years of neglect, and industry is cooperating, with tax incentives, for example, in France.

It is new, however, to find this thrust extending broadly into higher institutions, both in studies and admission policies. We have noted that credit is being extended to adults, particularly in Sweden and the United States, for work experience in terms of entrance qualifications to colleges and universities. Transfer is easier for students from technical institutes into higher institutions; most systems are concerned about mobility among the sectors, and are aware of the United States example in this regard where mobility has been encouraged by standard credit units among institutions.

Another pattern is alternating studies and work experience. Britain has its sandwich courses for this purpose, and now West Germany reports on what is considered a radical plan for a "Sandwich University" to alternate studies with practice. It is a "most radical break with the idea that university studies are a limited educational phase." The plan is characterized by catchwords like "life-long learning at intervals" and "change of places of learning." Such a concept is not likely to be realized; it will meet stubborn resistance from the state university system that, the authors say, can hardly be expected to experiment with concepts aimed not just at reform, but at changing radically the traditional university structure. Nevertheless, they conclude, it is a starting point for change in educational policy thinking.[28]

At the same time, in West Germany the concept of relating the practical program of *Fachhochschulen* to the theoretical and research studies of universities was basic to the creation of integrated comprehensive institutions. Although they have floundered in opposition and political party interests, and debate has waned from fatigue with reforms, the idea still prevails.

Professional training, traditionally followed by obligatory periods of practice for lawyers, doctors, and secondary school teachers in West Germany, is currently experimenting with the practice period earlier—while students are still studying at the university. There are moves in this direction in new licensing regulations for medicine, in teacher education at the University of Oldenburg, and similar efforts connecting natural and engineering sciences.

Internships and practice periods are not only spreading from the customary use following university medical training to other professions, but they are coming earlier in student training. Stressing performance criteria in evaluation of training accompanies the movement to incorporate practical experience into theoretical and more abstract periods of study. It is all part of the general thrust toward career preparation, vocational competence, and responsible professional practice that has the strong backing of governments everywhere.

The third direction of curricular change is toward multidisciplinary studies, another kind of knowledge application. Not necessarily involving practical experience, multidisciplinary approaches do ask for a test of knowledge insofar as they bring theoretical learning to bear on realistic issues. They are rather like proving the theorem—the abstract principles and knowledge projected—in the actual proof of solutions.

Solutions are wanted, above all, to the complex issues surrounding society. It is problem-solving that Mexico wants and needs; to this end, the new Metropolitan University was founded, and interdisciplinary studies have started in a number of Mexican universities. Thailand has established several institutes of contemporary social problems dealing with pressing current concerns like population growth and the environment. Moreover, in this case, universities took the initiative, not the centralized government.

There are plenty of recent examples, in the various countries, of special institutes, conferences, and seminars on contemporary issues, but not as many basic changes in universities to accommodate multidisciplinary studies. Of the five main directions for curricular change, efforts to relate separate disciplines, even for the sorely needed purpose of thie contributions to common issues of deep concern to society, seem to meet the most difficulties and constraints. Such efforts come directly at disciplinary, departmental walls that enclose faculty ground. Though the walls have been artificially constructed and arbitrarily set, they stand as the strongest obstacle to change, especially when it involves academic substance and style.

Newer universities seem to have the greatest chance. Five of Australia's new universities were deliberately innovative in this direction.

> Flinders, Macquarie, and La Trobe Universities all decided to break down the traditional barriers between disciplines and to cultivate interdisciplinary teaching and learning in 'schools of study.' Later Griffith and Murdoch Universites moved still further away from traditional academic disciplines by providing integrated programs based on major themes and problems.[29]

Bruce Williams explains that key planners for the new institutions were usually senior faculty from established universities, and "there was a desire to see something different, to provide genuine choice within the university sector." It could be that the senior staff seized the chance to make reforms that would probably never be adopted in their own universities. And beyond that, Williams adds, there were the forces of the knowledge explosion and the rapid growth in staff at Australian universities, which had reduced the average age of staff considerably and introduced different ideas with new-comers from North American academic backgrounds.

Yet, looking at the North American shores, one cannot easily identify where the courageous, interdisciplinary ideas came from. Quebec, perhaps. The *Université du Québec*, formed as a system from over a hundred normal schools and integrated with universities, has been well aware of its innovative role, and the colleges, new institutions, are not bound by traditions of the past. In order to get away from "disciplinism," the *Université* was structured:

> ...so that faculty would still be organized by departments, but students would be grouped by theme-oriented 'modules,' using departmental services, but involving both faculty and students in their planning and general operation. Such a structure was made possible by the fact the university with its constituents, even though they were in some cases largely a reorganization of existing institutions, was conceived by a group of young and dynamic planners, working essentially from outside the system. As it has turned out, the modular structure is still far from being generally accepted, one of the problems being that of harmonizing vertical and horizontal components.[30]

It seems doubtful that the ideas taking form in Australia's new universities came from the United States. A few experimental colleges, public as well as private, have organized with divisions of social sciences, humanities, and physical or natural sciences—not departments—but they tend to slip back toward the subject disciplines which faculty represent. There is, nevertheless, a growing practice among students of taking double majors and following related interests.

The United States pattern is somewhat like Britain's, only less substantial. Over the past four years or so, British universities generally have shown real growth in a "range of interdisciplinary degree programmes in all major subject areas," and colleges are diversifying "often in the direction of combined honours or interdisciplinary degrees." There are such examples across the whole span of older institutions in Britain.[31] The movement goes well beyond newer universities established for multidisciplinary studies like Sussex.

But the movement has not engulfed the Continent. West Germany has promoted project study which is viewed as the "most important and most radical attempt to change the conventional learning procedure." Based on learning by inquiry and developed through the initiative of students and teachers, projects concern:

> ...practical problems of social relevance that are related to the future
> occupations. The problem is to be "studied" by taking into consideration
> the resulting interdisciplinary perspectives and by using as many methods as
> possible.[32]

Initial attempts have met all the predictable obstacles of evaluating student performance, faculty teaching load, and coordinating the unconventional approach with standard, conventional procedures. It is hard to say whether such projects will receive wider application. At present, they are a "marginal and voluntary phenomenon of university life. Only at the newly founded University of Bremen have they become the basic organizational principle for studies."

France's approach was different. It started the reform structurally and legislated it nationally for universities. But multidisciplinary studies, one of the main aims of the reform, have turned out to be more a matter of intent than accomplishment. In the result, thus far, French universities seem to be about where the West German system is in this regard. The French Orientation Law was exceedingly general and compromising: "Universities are multidisciplinary and shall associate arts and letters with science and technology wherever possible. However, they may have a predominant interest."[33] The new UERs were a means of structural reorganization intended to further interdisciplinary cooperation, but many of them have remained disciplinary in base, and there is little noticeable development along the intended lines.

The West German and French systems are the ones out of step, or at least slower, in the movement toward more related studies. Sweden is with it. Many of the new Swedish institutions are not based on departments, and interdisciplinary structures are growing within older institutions. Bertil Östergren recalls from a Swedish study of innovation that:

> Changes in the cultural and social climate at the end of the 1960s loosened up traditional rigidities and were the basis for developing a problem and project orientation, interdisciplinarity, student-oriented curricula, social relevance, global responsibilities, and so on.[34]

It may be, midst the problems and pressures on higher education systems in the 1970s, that the effects of social criticism from students and the rest of society a decade ago have been underestimated. Curricular change is directed toward multidisciplinary studies and problem solving.

Reduction of time spent in study courses and professional preparation is the fourth direction toward which pressures are aimed, but progress in this direction is not marked. Unlike the emphasis on practical experience and multidisciplinary studies, concern for shorter study periods has not led to widespread curricular change or innovation. The issue, however, is being widely argued, and today financial costs and crowded conditions in some places are urging attention. Also, independent studies with students going at their own pace raise further questions about predetermined blocks of time set for certain types and stages of learning.

In the United States, undergraduate students have, for some time, been able to shorten the four-year college period. The practice is no longer unusual though it is not typical for the majority of students. Those who are exceptional can be accepted either for "early admission" to a college or university, meaning they skip the last year of secondary school, or for "advanced placement" which allows them to enter second-year college courses. Standardized tests are available across the country to measure achievement in particular subject fields and aid placement in college courses. There are a few cooperative programs that permit qualified students to enter professional schools in their last year of undergraduate study. Still the norm remains four years for undergraduate colleges and universities.

The issue of reduced study periods is heightened especially in West Germany because of the shortage of study places, the *numerus clausus* policy, and long lists of students awaiting entrance. Peisert and Framhein further observe that mass numbers in universities broke down personal contacts between faculty and students, and signs of disorientation have appeared in "prolonged periods of study, frequent changes of academic fields, and high drop-out rates."[35]

Of various corrective measures proposed, the Dahrendorf Plan generated the most heated controversy. Advocating three-year programs concentrating on teaching rather than research, the plan ran into heavy opposition: some critics charged it was too "school-like," others argued the labor market could not absorb the graduates and, anyway, employment favored the four-year graduate; and still others claimed graduates would lack the flexibility given by broad education and so fall prey to the "exploitations of capitalism." Needless to add, plans were stymied and later attempts to revive them have also failed.[36] Required study regulations, in West Germany, have been established in almost all disciplines, but they have not led to shortening study periods; quite the contrary, the total length of studies has been considerably increased.

Mexico, too, has tried reducing the duration of programs but, running into troubles, the plan was not widely adopted. Student reaction specifically to shortened *licenciatura* courses was resistant on the theory "that longer courses must be better."[37]

Set periods of time for medical, law, and other professional schools are also being debated in several countries and, on this level, controversy involves external pressures from practitioners. The U.K. report singles out some professional bodies as highly conservative barriers to worthwhile change. Australia mentions the influence on educational decisions from outside professional groups and cites an example indicating that the Institute of Engineers announced that from 1980 "a four-year degree course will be a condition of membership." This will have considerable impact on colleges offering engineering courses. Another instance is a decision by the leading accounting institute to make accounting a graduate profession.[38]

It is difficult enough to carry out reforms within the system, without additional pressures from professional association outside. Bruce Williams explains the long complicated series of negotiations that recast the under-graduate medical course at the universities of Sydney and New South Wales and reduced its length from six to five years. Initiated by faculty, the change involved financial considerations, numbers of students, courses in the university, increase in the medical teaching year, strains in the clinical years during changeover, and approvals from faculty and administrative bodies up to the federal University Commission.[39]

Efforts to condense study periods have not generally been successful, but several liberalizing influences are at work: the increasing number of adults enrolling and taking part-time couses, competency examinations for degrees and outside examiners, and the growth in independent learning which media will increase. All these forces question set time-periods and established routines in learning.

The fifth and most visible direction in curricular change is the use of new communication media that are just now beginning to show their efficacy in teaching and the learning process. Their introduction to the higher levels of education has been somewhat fearful and defensive. A few imaginative minds championed the potential and bravely purchased physical equipment, but many hopes were unrealistic in the early days of audiovisual technologies and "hardware" was stacked away in closets.

So goes the story in the United States. Although the Ford Foundation's early gamble on "Continental Classroom" in the late 1950s attracted considerable notice, it did not spark other national television ventures. Yet, in the first week of the course on modern physics taught by an eminent professor from Berkeley, some 5,000 students enrolled for credit, 250 colleges and universites extended credit based on their own examinations, and an estimated 270,000 persons daily viewed the course.[40] The Classroom continued several years with other courses on chemistry and mathematics.

Since that time, the use of television and radio has been largely on a regional basis, but its usage has steadily increased, and novelty is wearing off. The University of Maryland has experimented since 1972 and enrolled over 13,500 persons in courses. The University of Mid-America serves some 10,000 students in several states; Miami-Dade and Chicago community colleges both extensively employ the media; and many others have more limited usage through closed circuit facilities, audio-visual technologies in classrooms, taped courses, and so on.

Canada's adoptions of such new forms of instruction is along lines similar to those in the United States, but not so extensive. Some innovative methods in Western provices were mentioned earlier; Quebec has the Télè-université (the title is etymological—education at a distance), but television itself has accounted for less than 8 percent of activities; Ontario has the TVO network, but its main purpose is quality entertainment and public affairs programs, like the United States Public Broadcasting Corporation. Neither is to compete with post-secondary institutions nor to offer instruction as a first purpose. Ontario's network has presented courses only twice and recognizes its function as supplementary to regular instruction. For the most complete innovative use of television, along with radio, cassettes, telephones, and travelling tutors, one must look to the Memorial University in the Atlantic provinces. There, the extension program goes well beyond those in other provinces, although it serves only a local area.[41]

According to Tony Becher, Britain made a rather halting start with educational television in the latter half of the 1960s, despite the powerful and impressive backing of an official UGC committee on the use of audio-visual aids. Closed circuit television was the most familiar form. Leeds University and others set up well-equipped centers that have turned out to be "little more than a marginal embellishment" for undergraduate teaching. The same thing was happening to other technical innovations, and seldom was material designed as a learning resource transferred from one institution to another.[42]

Nonetheless, it is instructive to note that, in those same years of the late sixties in Britain, planning and preparation were rolling ahead at a rapid rate for the Open University, which admitted its first class of 25,000 students in 1971. Political forces had gathered around Harold Wilson's notion that the media could give working classes a second chance at an education. In fact, it was in a 1963 campaign speech that Wilson first advocated a "university of the air" and, after his election, the idea took root in the Department of Education and Science under the leadership of Jennie Lee, who was then undersecretary.[43]

From its inception, the Open University (OU) has been separate from the binary system, both the "private" or "autonomous" sector of universities and the "public" sector of polytechnics, colleges of education, and further education. Its separation may be one reason for its remarkable success; it was neither hampered by inherited forms and customs in the established system nor grafted on to an already existent institution. The Open had the whole job to do afresh, with no special pattern to follow. At least, it avoided the fate of being an embellishment, marginal, or supplementary to an ongoing institution. Although some of its critics may still consider it to be just that to the regular system of British higher education, nevertheless the Open's degrees are accepted as comparable with those of conventional universities, which are increasingly accepting OU credites for transfer students and using OU courses for their own students.

The Open University, by far the most daring media innovation yet to emerge, has achieved status not only at home; the model has been adopted in large part by many other countries and it has stimulated adaptations on smaller scales. Japan's University of the Air, planned by the Ministry of Education and the Broadcasting Corporation, will offer the bachelor's degree based on five years of study, including some institutional instruction and an examination. A nationwide survey estimates that as many as 450,000 students may use the university.[44] It awaits legislative action.

After several limited trials with Open University course materials and much debate over whether such a concept would be successful in the United States, a new National University Consortium has appeared. It is a joint venture of seven colleges and universities and eleven television stations that carry the courses received via satellite. Tutorials are optional and most of the student's work is done at home. Courses are on the undergraduate level, leading to a bachelor's degree in about six years. The consortium is patterned after the OU, but with one major difference: students must enroll and pay tuition at a participating institution which awards the credit and degree.

Thailand's Office of University Affairs is starting a new open university that utilizes integrated media and facilitates independent study. It is home-based for participants in rural areas as well as urban, and the dual target is both knowledge and skills.[45] Before the revolution, plans were laid for the Free University of Iran and the Radio and Television Institute to provide learning opportunities, especially for post-secondary education in remote parts of the country and for those waiting to enter regular institutions. Televised courses, supplemented by regular classroom lectures, were to be in science, teacher training, and health care.[46]

The value of the media, with necessary support services, is, of course, enormous for developing countries. Just as they can leap forward to air travel, so they can skip some unnecessary construction and go to universities without walls and to air waves for radio and television instruction.

West Germany introduced "Extension Studies Through Media" as a broad pilot project in 1977–78, offering first-year courses in biology, electronics, mathematics, and psychology. Progress in its development was slow due to difficulties in the cooperation of Länder and the media, and lack of interest from the higher education institutions.

It was easier to launch an extension university in Hagen (North Rhine Westphalia) along the more customary pattern of a network of study centers. More than 10,000 students were enrolled by the third year in 30 centers. Contrary to the original purpose of serving students excluded by *numerus clausus*, however, mainly adults enrolled and three-fourths of the students in 1976 had already finished their professional training.[47] Britain's OU had a comparable experience; instead of attracting workers and miners as intended, the first class had about one-third teachers, just under 4 percent workers (mostly from electrical, metal, manufacturing and related industries), and the remainder from the professions, the arts, scientists and technicians, engineers, housewives, and clerical employees.[48]

The research and development organization in Sweden was also to further the use of educational technology, but research turned instead to social and organizational matters. Later, after considering the idea of an open university, Sweden decided against it. The country already had an extensive adult education program. So, extension services have been extended farther through university study circles operating in some 24 cities; and the new law provides additional services for students working at home through mail or telephone contact with tutors and attendance on a few weekends at an institution.

Poland's use of television, teaching machines, and other technologies has lagged even though approved and assisted by the authorities, but general extension studies have been expanded with consultation points throughout the country where teachers and extramural students meet for courses and seminars. Established institutions have also set up many branches in small towns, and, most recently, in industrial plants.

Certain hypotheses are tenable concerning the use of communicative media in higher education:

- Where the media have been employed most effectively, the organization and direction have come from outside the higher education system, and remained outside in the operational phase. No large scale program has yet been incorporated in an established system.

- Existent institutions, faculty, and administrators have been exceedingly reluctant even to experiment with the new media. Hence, the media have played, at best, only a supplementary part that could be easily discarded. Projects have worked best when conceived *de novo*.
- Too often, acquisition of the machinery of communications, the hardware, has been pursued with resultant neglect to the "software"—the content and substance. Techniques must be recognized as merely accessory to the foremost purpose of content and chosen for what they can add to the message being conveyed.
- Use of the media in higher education has just begun. Its possibilities are very great in solving some of the problems in instruction, and in making education available to people of any age, at any place, and at any time.

In the various reports on innovation, flexibility, and change from the dozen countries in this study, there is one major item missing: references to computer-assisted instruction. Surely it is not taken for granted; it is too new. Yet, computerized processes are already in use throughout the world of business. Libraries and research centers are rapidly becoming dependent on them. Storage capacities for information and facts are tremendous, and can revolutionize scholarship. Pupils in elementary and secondary schools are increasingly using computers in self-instruction.

Where are higher education systems in this development? Instruction in computer languages is available in first-rate universities. The physical sciences have discovered the computer's value in research. Many systems are computerized in business and financial matters; there is not, however, corresponding use in instruction. Teaching continues as always through lectures, seminars, and tutorials. Students who are used to computerized learning are going to be entering higher education in ever growing numbers. Universities cannot relegate the computer to a new "department" with teachers in computer language. Why are the powers of imaginative projection and use so wanting in the creative minds of educators?

Regardless of omissions and obstacles in higher education systems, new means of communication are used increasingly throughout societies and in homes of people around the world. In many ways, classrooms are moving into homes where people study independently and use new media, as well as the traditional means of books, assignments, and papers under guidance of teachers—at a distance. The trend is unmistakable and gaining momentum.

Whether it is called the Open University in Britain, Free University in Iran, University of the Air in Japan, Everyman's University in Israel, or whatever, the pattern is rapidly spreading. In the same direction, independent studies, universities without walls, extension programs, and study centers are growing and moving to the people. It is a tremendous change that will naturally, in the course of time, be felt in many ways by established higher education systems.

The preponderant forces for adjustment and new directions are from outside the system and confront its accustomed ways. Some responses are evident within the systems, especially from teachers in the classroom in terms of how they are teaching and the content of courses. Other more dramatic responses are seen in alternative programs and the use of media and technological aids. The changing curricular directions at present may well hold the greatest challenge for higher education in the last decades of the twentieth century.

10
EPILOGUE

During the past 30 years, the biggest changes in higher education have come from the massive numbers of people entering post-secondary schools with the encouragement and aid of government. In fact, it was more than encouragement from government; in most instances, it was initiative. Not many educators in the developed countries were pressuring their governments for public policies to enable mass entrance. The pressures came from outside the higher education establishment just as the forces for major change continue to be external to the ongoing institutions. That may well be a general characteristic of social institutions. Once established, their concern centers on the continuance of present purposes.

Before the Second World War, higher education was a closely knit enclave with well-worn customs and traditions. *Elite* is the word to describe the professors and students. The magnitude of the change that has occurred is staggering. And it has come so quickly that many of us have not stopped to assess carefully the trends that have emerged.

This study of higher education systems in 12 different countries has provided indicators of the dominant trends and the problems that accompany them. The function of this concluding chapter is to summarize these trends and comment on the problems.

Foremost is the trend increasing the powers of government, where the greatest portion, if not all, of the funding resides. The movement is toward centralized power, but not always at the national level. In the federally organized countries, the balance of power rests uneasily on either the state (provincial) or the national level. At the present time in Canada, the center of power is provincial; in the United States, the states have greatly increased powers, and the national government has also entered into higher education areas like admission policies and appointment practices which hitherto have been considered out of bounds. Government powers in the Federal Republic of Germany have increased at both Länder and Bund levels; and in Australia the shift is markedly to the Commonwealth.

Among the countries that already had national, centralized governments, the power center has generally grown in its influence. Only Sweden has made a real effort to decentralize and share some power with regional bodies, but the significance of that action remains to be seen. Legislation in France, calling for a similar type of decentralization, has not been implemented. Unless a decisive position in allocating finances is awarded the regional group, such structural changes mean little. In other centralized states—Japan, Thailand, and Britain—the power of central ministries dealing with higher education is increasing. Regardless of the political organization in the various countries, the position of government has become more dominant and its actions more directive in higher education affairs.

It is curious that this trend toward government's increasingly centralized control has occurred just as higher education systems are experiencing democratization in internal governance. Inside the system, many more people are involved in decision making, and innumerable interests are represented; it is a time of participation for everybody in everything. Theoretically, the two trends—democratization and centralization—might be expected to collide at some point or counterbalance each other and check undue influence by either force.

Thus far, however, instead of colliding or counterbalancing, the two forces are moving together at least in loose alliance. Insofar as government's action is responsive to the people's perceived interest, the alliance may continue. But one thing is certain: the combined trends of democratization within institutions and government's increasingly dominant role have politicized higher education systems. This is particularly true of the European systems, notably Sweden, France, and West Germany. Though it may not yet be so obvious in some other countries, the trend is there. Compared with a few decades ago when higher education was on the periphery or even outside of the political arena, the change is startling.

The alliance of student demand and government concern expressed in legislation and funding has also introduced new academic trends. Beyond mass education itself, the thrust currently is toward career and vocational preparation, credit for practical work experience, and performance criteria. Adults are becoming students, especially on a part-time basis in some of the countries, and continuing education is the developing pattern. And new types of institutions and programs have been created to accommodate the new demands.

Universities, the starting point for the expansion, seem like an island surrounded by relatively new institutions offering training and educational programs to meet the changing needs. Community colleges have appeared, polytechnics and *Fachhochschulen* have emerged, institutes for technical and advanced education have proliferated, and so on. The great expansion is now in these institutions, and public monies, following the number of students, are flowing to such programs. Universities face growing competition for funds, within higher education systems as well as without, from other public services.

The growth in institutional types has led to the development of sectors in higher education and the concept of systems. Governments want to see the comprehensive picture, the whole spectrum of educational opportunities available to the population. They want planning on a scale larger than sectors, and coordination or rationalization of the different parts.

At the moment, this seems the hardest of tasks. Individual sectors like universites, or colleges of advanced education, or technical institutes are well aware of what their sister or brother institutions are doing, and they are related within sectors in governing structures and professional associations. But no one is very knowledgeable about what his cousins are doing in a different sector. The relatives meet infrequently, and individual interests remain closer to home base. It is on the overall family level that the links are needed and that the welfare of the whole group needs to be promoted through its related interests. The total view is too often missing.

From government's point of view, based on financial realities and common sense, planning and coordination are essential. A look at higher education readily reveals duplicated programs and services, waste is apparent, and disparate parts of higher education systems exist visibly without defined purposes. So the trend is toward coordination to put the system in order and get its parts functioning more cooperatively and efficiently. In this effort particularly, governmental intervention is shown to be increasing in areas formerly left to institutional autonomy.

Not only has government adopted stronger policies to further coordination in higher education, but it is also noticeably strengthening measures for general accountability in many respects. In countries where the economy is not flourishing and inflation runs high, financial exigency strengthens the concern for evidence of expenditures and effective performance. The trend toward more thorough accountability clashes in many instances with the age-old principle of autonomy in higher education affairs. Regulations are becoming onerous in administrative operations and they are also eroding autonomy in the more academic areas.

Exceptions to the trend are the Swedish and, to some extent, the French higher education systems. Having most highly centralized and controlled systems, they are attempting to rebuild autonomy in institutions within the system. It will be interesting to see if either country is at all successful in the attempt. Other nations, however, could well examine the reasons for this reverse movement after having achieved a high degree of central control and uniformity. It raises questions about the desirability of the movement underway in the other nations, and whether limits should be imposed to prevent overachievement in the effort to gain order, coordination, and accountability in higher education systems.

Accountability inevitably means a justification of activities and, at minimum, an explanation of performance. Lines are tightening in what was, for a long time, a relatively free state of affairs with little governmental intervention in administration. This is no longer generally true. As the oldest type of higher education, universities in particular are aware of the reins being applied. Institutions in the other newer sectors that have been formed closer to local or regional authorities naturally do not feel so strongly about it. They are accustomed to controls and accountability.

Tensions have risen between government and universities over questions of autonomy and the presence of public authority. From statements in country reports, such issues seem more acute in Canada, the United States, and West Germany than in other countries. The adversarial stance is lamentable for both sides. Actual free speech is not at issue. None of the countries raises that question, although Poland's "flying university" is reputed to have started because some subjects considered vital were not allowed in the approved curriculum.

Centralized systems of higher education, including universities, have long been used to formal procedures for approval of curriculum, appointments, admission standards, degree requirements, budgetary practices, and so on. Yet institutional autonomy has existed in the daily operations of academic life, and it continues to operate in many respects today in most of our countries. Therefore, it is most important, on the one side, for universities to sort out the issues involved in real autonomy and not raise the cry indiscriminately over every procedural change enacted. On the other side, government authorities dealing with universities and other sectors of higher education systems must consider more carefully the implications of their judgements and regulations. Often officials are unaware of the effects of their decisions and even unaware of the total power they may wield. They must, in their turn, sort out the possibilities to find those most helpful to the systems and potentially the least negative in effect.

As long as the government personnel usually came from the academic ranks, these problems were not so significant; understanding prevailed. But as more government positions are being filled outside academe, and consultation with educators does not always occur before decisive action is taken, the issues are multiplying and dangers to the healthy functioning of higher education systems begin to appear. Cooperative arrangements and agreements must be reached by working together with common purpose and concern for the improvement of higher education.

Given the general belief in higher education and democratic government, these issues can be solved. The situation, however, will worsen if governments act irresponsibly by chance, through ignorance, or for temporary political gains. Similar results may be anticipated if higher education systems respond unreasonably to legitimate requests and act irresponsibly in ordering their own affairs. Combining energies to work on substantial problems can help.

Governments and higher education should, above all, focus their attention and joint efforts on improving the *quality* of higher education and strengthening *diversity* in the systems. These are the crucial areas now and for the future.

Quality has been directly affected by mass enrollments and the rapid employment of teachers. In many countries, students who are less well prepared have been entering higher education in increasing numbers. Courses and methods of teaching that had evolved for a smaller select group have not automatically proved their effectiveness with the large mixed audience. Adjustments have been made and changes introduced, but standards have depreciated in many cases, and the quality of academic achievement has been lowered.

Some hold that "meritocracy" is the antidote for the malaise and the way to restore standards. This implies raising standards and creating greater competition from which the most talented academically will rise, and higher selectivity will seep through the whole system at every level, from entrance requirements through graduation. While this approach may serve the fortunate few, it is not a practical cure for the ailing standards which affect the majority of students. Moreover, we know that socioeconomic factors are at work as well as genes in determining student's abilities and accomplishments. In democratic societies, the answer has to lie in developing new standards in a broader range of fields that recognize different abilities and their contributions to society.

Furthermore, it is well to remember with some humility that the larger numbers of people enrolling may simply have exposed shortcomings in higher education that already existed, even though the numbers also led to other new deficiencies. There is increasing use of competency examinations not only to credit independent and experiential learning, but also to check on what was learned in more orthodox ways in traditional institutions. Performance criteria are advocated to determine if studies were adequate for the tasks to be done.

Standards cannot be effectively legislated; they are better instilled in students when strongly held by teachers, supported by colleagues and administrators. Quality, in the final analysis, is a standard demanded by teachers who are well prepared and able. The emphasis on teaching reported from many countries is an encouraging indicator of the concern for quality and improvement. Whether the concern will be translated into active efforts to improve teaching is the important point.

Excluding Sweden's inservice training for teachers, faculty development programs of any size are notably absent in the various higher education systems. Quality remains a pious assertion in most cases. And treatises on higher education generally call for improvement of quality, but stop there; they suggest few ways to do it.

Ideas for improvement are not likely to come from government offices or, if they do, the programs may not be very suitable to the academic terrain. Rather than invite such intervention, higher education institutions and systems would do well to scrutinaize their own internal practices and standards with an eye toward self-improvement. Much can be done in this particular area without additional finances. Since money is at issue in many countries, it is harder today to get financing for faculty development programs that involve released time or additional staff. Nevertheless, such proposals should be made to the funding source; their very uniqueness could bring favorable reaction and support.

Educational research in the process of learning and optimal conditions for it has had little effect on the quality and improvement of teaching. Such research has been going on in the United States and Sweden for some time, and of late, centers have been established in Japan and West Germany. But conclusions thus far are mostly additions to the mystery of the learning process. Results do not make their way into significant experimental programs on a scale large enough to influence the general pattern and practices. Research conclusions are either inconclusive or ignored.

Emphasis on the need to improve methods and the quality of teaching does not mean the present situation is very bad or hopeless. To the contrary, there are high quality institutions in every higher education system, and academic standards have their protectors. One of the best protective devices is Britain's Council for National Academic Awards (CNAA). Although established by the government, the CNAA is another of those British inventions that seem to belong to the academics. Panels are drawn from universities and polytechnics, and the operation is staffed largely by academic peers. Their task is to approve new courses for degree credit, to maintain the academic gold standard and preserve the claim for equivalency of degrees throughout Britain. For courses already being offered, the system has its custom of external examiners which has been very effective in checking on the standards of academic achievement. Other countries could well consider this practice to raise or protect the quality of work. Official administrative channels for approval may not be sufficient.

The range of quality from excellent to poor is great in the United States system. Moreover, as competition for students grows in a period of declining enrollments, there is justified worry over standards being lowered at entrance and for retention of students on whom financing depends. Accrediting agencies, supported by the institutions, are not as severe and demanding as they should be. There is no higher education system without this type of problem. Developing nations have it to an extreme degree, and by studying practices elsewhere, they could conceivably protect standards while their systems are still in the formative stage.

Diversity within higher education systems is the other major area where the concerted efforts of governments and systems are most needed. When the commitment to mass enrollment and universal education was made, it followed naturally that increased diversity of study programs would be required; more people, more different interests, and more variation in types of abilities. We saw alternative institutions created and institutions merged and refashioned during the great expansion.

Now, as we face the issues of better planning and coordination, it is essential to differentiate standards according to the purposes of higher education in each sector, and not to drift mindlessly into imitative patterns. Genuine equality—not identity—of functions must be recognized and accepted; the superficiality of hierarchy must be rejected. The distinctiveness of substance and appropriate methods in the various study programs are the issue, not false notions of positions on a scale of influence. Somehow it is assumed that to lift an institution's status to the college or university level is to upgrade its standards. Diversity of purpose and function gets lost, but presumably quality gains. Maybe it is too much to ask that "academic drift" be revealed for what it too frequently is—academic snobbery at its most insidious level. This humanly infectious disease, of course, is not unknown to the other professions.

The development of comprehensive institutions, which is happening in many systems around the world, brings its own hazards for diversity. Broader curricula lap over on each side into the territories of technical and vocational programs and universities. If only cooperative arrangements, student mobility, and faculty exchange could take place without total amalgamation, diversity and clear purpose might endure in the separate sectors. But comprehensive institutions are seen as means to coordinate and, above all, to increase efficiency. Those are powerful motivational forces that are not necessarily on the lookout to preserve diversity.

Similarly, the drive for conformity which makes administration easier and some people more comfortable threatens diversity. Procedural standardization both within and across sectoral lines of higher education systems is most tempting to achieve organizational order from what often appears as chaotic academic affairs. Procedures establish ways of doing things and can stifle innovation.

Uniformity is achieved at inestimable cost to the education process which at its unhampered best is creative and highly individual in styles of teaching and learning. If diversity is to be preserved and increased to provide for the untold interests and abilities of man—the great learning potential— then the also human tendency to organize affairs to the point of uniformity must be wisely controlled and examined carefully at each step to strengthen the differentiation within higher education systems.

It would be a wry situation indeed if uniformity stifles higher education systems just as diversity sprouts in nontraditional modes of education. Universities without walls are being born at an expanding rate through media and technology, through communications, cassettes and tapes in homes equipped with books and study guides. Much of this infusion of higher education into people's lives has occurred thus far without, or in spite of, higher education systems. Diversity may be so assured, but quality may again be threatened. The open market selling of higher education promises to shatter still further the walls of universities and extend the definition of higher education beyond the present systems' wavering boundaries.

Of the many issues confronting higher education systems in today's world and the foreseeable future, none are more crucial than the improvement of quality and the strengthening of diversity. On these pervasive issues the systems and their governments should join together to enhance opportunities for all of their people.

Notes

Note: Almost all references are to the series of 12 country reports on which this book is based. Each is published under the common title *Systems of Higher Education*: (*name of country*) (New York: International Council for Educational Development, 1978). A complete list of countries and authors is given below. To simplify notes after that, reference is made only to the country report and page numbers. The author's name is included where parts of the report are attributed to particular authors.

Systems of Higher Education:

Australia. Bruce Williams.

Canada. Edward Sheffield, Duncan Campbell, Jeffrey Holmes, B. B. Kymlicka, and James Whitelaw.

Federal Republic of Germany. Hansgert Peisert and Gerhild Framhein.

France. Alain Bienaymé.

Iran. M. Reza Vaghefi, Dariush Nowrasteh, and Abdol Hossein Samii.

Japan. Katsuya Narita.

Mexico. Alfonso Rangel Guerra.

Poland. Jan Szczepański.

Sweden. Rune Premfors and Bertil Östergren.

Thailand. Sippanondha Ketudat and Wichit Srisa-an.

United Kingdom. Tony Becher, Jack Embling, and Maurice Kogan.

United States. Alan Pifer, John Shea, David D. Henry, and Lyman Glenny.

CHAPTER 1

1. *Iran*, pp. 1–2.
2. *The World Almanac and Book of Facts 1980* (New York: Newspaper Enterprise Association 1979), pp. 513–98.
3. *Thailand*, p. 10.
4. *Japan*, p. 12.
5. *Sweden*, Rune Premfors, p. 38.
6. *The World Almanac*, op. cit. Also the entry on each country in the *Encyclopedia Britannica* (Chicago: Encyclopedia Britannica, 1974). Many of the countries have relatively smaller numbers of people from different ethnic bases that are not included in this general text. For example, although Sweden's population is very homogeneous, there are some 10,000 Lapps and four other groups (Finnish, Serbo-Croation, Turkish, and Greek) since World War II that live in separate communities and wish instruction in their own languages. Japan has about one million Korean and Chinese people as well as a small indigenous minority of Ainu people. Thailand has some 40,000 Vietnamese who fled their country 30 years ago during the first Indo-China war and currently there are many refugees from the recent Vietnam war, and Cambodia.
7. *Canada*, Edward Sheffield, p. 2.-
8. See John Millett's essay "Planning and Management in National Structures," in *12 Systems of Higher Education: 6 Decisive Issues* (New York: International Council for Educational Development, 1978), pp. 13–16. He discusses three governmental variables: socio-political structure in two broad categories of monolithic and pluralistic forms; organizational arrangements of unitary and federal power; and economic stages of developed or developing countries.

CHAPTER 2

1. Clark Kerr, "Goals for Higher Education: Elusive and Sometimes Treacherous," in *12 Systems of Higher Education: 6 Decisive Issues* (New York: International Council for Educational Development, 1978), pp. 2–3.
2. *United Kingdom*, Tony Becher, pp. 89–90. See Chapter 7, "Achievement of Purposes," pp. 89–109.
3. *Poland*, p. 24.
4. *Sweden*, Rune Premfors, pp. 55–56. See the full discussion of goals, pp. 55–62.
5. *Mexico*, pp. 8–10. There is some discrepancy between numbers in the original text and Table 6, but the conclusion drawn is substantially correct.
6. *Iran*, pp. 17–21. The reader will notice an error in the original text stating "metallurgical" engineers when I assume it should have been, according to Table 4, "general" engineers.
7. *Thailand*, p. 24.
8. *Poland*, p. 24.
9. *United Kingdom*, Jack Embling, pp. 31–33. See the full chapter, pp. 31–37.
10. *Canada*, Edward Sheffield, p. 13.
11. *Japan*, pp. 13, 16.
12. *Sweden*, Rune Premfors, pp. 61–62.
13. *Federal Republic of Germany*, pp. 5–6.
14. *Sweden*, Rune Premfors, p. 61.
15. *Poland*, p. 4.
16. Ibid, p. 7.

17. *Federal Republic of Germany*, p. 12.
18. *Poland*, p. 11.
19. *Sweden*, Rune Premfors, p. 20.
20. U. S. Bureau of the Census, *Current Population Reports*, Series P-20, No. 335. "School Enrollment—Social and Economic Characteristics of Students: October 1978 (Advance report)." (Washington, D. C.: Government Printing Office, 1979), p. 5.
21. *France*, pp. 4–5.
22. *Australia*, p. 3.
23. *Canada*, Edward Sheffield, pp. 4–6.
24. *Japan*, pp. 24–25, 12, 15.
25. *France*, pp. 3–5.
26. *Federal Republic of Germany*, p. 15.
27. *Sweden*, Rune Premfors, pp. 6–7.
28. *Mexico*, p. 21.
29. *Iran*, p. 14.
30. *Australia*, p. 69.
31. *Canada*, Edward Sheffield, p. 207.
32. David Anderson, "Polish Underground University Teaches Banned Subjects" in *The New York Times*, July 23, 1978, p. 3. Also see John Darnton, "Poland repressing 'Flying University,'" November 30, 1979, p. A8.
33. *Thailand*, p. 26.
34. *Canada*, Edward Sheffield, pp. 16, 206.
35. *United Kingdom*, Jack Embling, pp. 32, 34–35.
36. *Mexico*, pp. 17–18.
37. *Poland*, p. 24.
38. *Federal Republic of Germany*, p. 5.
39. *Sweden*, Rune Premfors, p. 58.
40. *Mexico*, p. 18.
41. *Australia*, p. 38.
42. *United States*, John Shea, p. 39.
43. *Thailand*, pp. 24, 115.
44. *Australia*, p. 33.
45. Ibid., p. 38.
46. *Poland, p. 25.*
47. *United Kingdom*, Jack Embling, p. 36.
48. *Sweden*, Rune Premfors, pp. 58–59.
49. *Canada*, Edward Sheffield, pp. 16, 207.
50. *France*, pp. 121–122 (Title I, Article 2).
51. From the Appendix, "Statements on Goals," in *12 Systems of Higher Education*, op. cit., p. 203.
52. John O'Leary, "Five-year plan to emphasize Third World issues" in *Times Higher Education Supplement*, No. 351, August 4, 1978, p. 4.
53. Malcolm G. Scully, "A New Era of Concern for International Education" in *The Chronicle of Higher Education*, Vol. XVI, No. 21, July 31, 1978, p. 1.
54. *Poland*, p. 25.

CHAPTER 3

1. Barbara Burn, *Higher Education in Nine Countries* (New York: McGraw-Hill, 1971), p. 14.
2. *Iran*, pp. 6–8.

3. *Thailand*, pp. 8–9, 11, 13, 16–17.

4. Ibid., p. 31.

5. *Mexico*, pp. 6–11.

6. *Japan*, pp. 24–26, 73–76.

7. Ibid., pp. 53–54, 78.

8. Ibid., pp. 79–80.

9. Susan C. Nelson, "Financial Trends and Issues," in *Public Policy and Private Higher Education*, ed. David W. Breneman and Chester E. Finn, Jr. (Washington, D.C.: The Brookings Institution, 1978), pp. 104–5. Figures used are for academic year 1973–74, the most recent available for the items included.

10. *United States*, John Shea, p. 20.

11. Japan also has tax exemption for contributors to private schools and colleges, but it operates differently from the United States. The Japan Private School Promotion Foundation has a Committee of Examination of Contributors which investigates contributions and, if they are cleared, "the contribution from a corporation is tax exempt, whereas a contribution by an individual is tax exempt only beyond the first ten thousand yen." See Tsunesaburo Tokoyama, "Japanese System of Indirect Support to Private Institutions, in *Higher Education in the World Community*, ed. Stephen K. Bailey (Washington, D. C.: American Council on Education, 1977), p. 1974.

12. *France*, pp. 64, 84.

13. From remarks by Professor Larkin Kerwin of the Université Laval in Quebec at the Commonwealth Universities' Congress in Vancouver. Reported in the *Times Higher Education Supplement*, September 1, 1978, p. 6.

14. Ibid., p. 6, from remarks by Professor Bruce Williams, vice-chancellor of the University of Sydney, Australia.

15. *Mexico*, p. 9. See also Table 7.

16. *Canada*, Edward Sheffield, p. 17.

17. Ibid., pp. 28–29.

18. Benson Wilson, "Comments to the Canadian Society for Studies in Higher Education." (Unpublished, May 30, 1978).

19. Ken Whittingham, "Quebec's Universities Bristle at Suggestion of Public Control," in *The Chronicle for Higher Education*, September 11, 1978, pp. 13–14.

20. *United States*, p. 12.

21. Ibid., p. 114. See the section on federal government, pp. 112–16.

22. *Federal Republic of Germany*, p. 85. See the section on finance, pp. 85–92.

23. Ibid., p. 190.

24. John Millett, "Planning and Management in National Structures," in *12 Systems of Higher Education: 6 Decisive Issues* New York: International Council for Educational Development, 1978), pp. 45–48.

25. *Iran*, p. 13.

26. *Canada*, Edward Sheffield, p. 22.

CHAPTER 4

1. *Poland, pp. 32–36.*

2. *Sweden*, Rune Premfors, pp. 81–84.

3. *Japan*, pp. 51–52.

4. *Sweden*, Rune Premfors, pp. 77–78.

5. *Federal Republic of Germany*, p. 60.

6. Ibid., p. 61.

7. Ibid., p. 66.

8. Ibid., pp. 63–67.

9. *Japan*, p. 52.

10. *Federal Republic of Germany*, p. 57.

11. Ibid., pp. 55–56.

12. *Mexico,* pp. 25–26.

CHAPTER 5

1. Burton Clark, "Coordination: Patterns and Processes, in *12 Systems of Higher Education: 6 Decisive Issues* (New York: International Council for Educational Development, 1978), pp. 57–95.

2. *Federal Republic of Germany*, p. 190.

3. John Anwyl, "Towards a Co-ordinated National System of Tertiary Education: Some Problems of Development in a Federal System," (Unpublished paper delivered at Fourth International Conference on Higher Education, University of Lancanster, England, August 29–September 1, 1978), p. 3.

4. *Australia*, p. 4.

5. Ibid., p. 7.

6. Caryl P. Haskins, *Of Societies and Men* (New York: Viking Press, 1960), p. 46.

7. Ibid., p. 107.

8. Steven Rattner, "Carter Announces Legislative Plan to Revise U. S. Regulatory Process," *The New York Times,* March 26, 1979, p. A1.

9. *Sweden*, Rune Premfors, p. 88.

10. Ibid., p. 43.

11. Steven Rattner, op. cit., p. A1.

12. Burton R. Clark, "The Insulated Americans: Five Lessons from Abroad," *Change Magazine*, (November, 1978), p. 25. See the entire article, pp. 24–30.

13. *Thailand*, p. 54.

14. *Japan*, Appendix I. pp. 100–1, 126–27.

15. *Federal Republic of Germany*, p. 184. See also pp. 40–46.

16. Daniel Levy, "Comparative Perspectives on Academic Governance in Mexico," (Unpublished paper presented to Yale Higher Education Research Group, Institution for Social and Policy Studies, Yale University, New Haven, Connecticut, 1978), p. 12.

17. *Canada*, Edward Sheffield, p. 194. Although Canada has formally named coordination as a function of such national departments as the Ministry of State for Science and Technology and the Secretary of State, the operating headquarters for coordinative activities are in the provincial departments of education.

18. *Canada*, B. B. Kymlicka, pp. 107–115.

19. *Canada*, Jeffrey Holmes, pp. 43–47.

20. *Education Amendments of 1972: Conference Report*, 92nd Congress, Report No. 92-1085 (Government Printing Office, Washington, D. C.), pp. 93–94. See also *United States*, John Shea, pp. 34–36.

21. *United States*, David D. Henry, pp. 68–69.

22. *Canada*, B. B. Kymlicka, pp. 108–9.

23. Ibid., p. 107.

24. *France*, p. 29.

25. *United Kingdom*, Jack Embling, p. 22.

26. *Federal Republic of Germany*, pp. 32–33.

27. John H. Van de Graaff and Dorotea Furth, "France," in *Academic Power, Patterns of*

Authority in Seven National Systems of Higher Education by John H. Van de Graaff, Burton R. Clark, Dorotea Furth, et al. (New York: Praeger Publishers, 1978), pp. 60–61.

28. Rune Premfors, "The Politics of Higher Education in Sweden: Recent Developments (1976–1978)," (Unpublished paper presented to Yale Higher Education Research Group Institution for Social and Policy Studies, Yale University, New Haven, Connecticut, 1978), p. 6. See pp. 2–8 and 17–18 for discussion of regional boards reflected in this section of text.

29. *Sweden*, Rune Premfors, pp. 47–48.

30. Ibid., pp. 103–4.

31. Rune Premfors, op. cit., p. 18.

32. *Sweden*, Rune Premfors, p. 104.

33. Ibid.

CHAPTER 6

1. *Federal Republic of Germany*, p. 190.

2. From an unpublished addendum by John Elmendorf to Alfonse Rangel Guerra, *Systems of Higher Education: Mexico* (New York: ICED, 1978).

3. *Sweden*, Rune Premfors, pp. 129–30.

4. *Federal Republic of Germany*, p. 191.

5. Ibid., p. 6.

6. *France*, p. 84.

7. *Canada*, B. B. Kymlicka, p. 117.

CHAPTER 7

1. Poland, p. 13, See "Selection of Students," pp. 12–15.

2. *United States*, Alan Pifer, pp. 1–5. See also Larry G. Simon, *Access Policy and Procedures and the Law in U. S. Higher Education* (New York: International Council for Higher Education, 1978), especially pp. 29–36. For further information on the United States and the Federal Republic of Germany, see other books in the ICED's Access series: Willi Becker, *Barriers to Higher Education in the Federal Republic of Germany* (New York: ICED, 1977); Ulrich Teichler; *Admission to Higher Education in the United States, A German Critique* (New York: ICED, 1978); and *Access to Higher Education: Two Perspectives. Final Report of the German–U. S. Study Group* (New York, ICED, 1978).

3. *Sweden*, Rune Premfors, pp. 106–8.

4. Ibid., pp. 105–6.

5. *Federal Republic of Germany*, p. 93. See the section "Admission of Students," pp. 92–98. Also see Will Becker, op. cit.

6. Ibid., p. 95.

7. Ibid., p. 96–97. I have followed the report closely in describing West Germany's complicated system.

8. Ibid., p. 98. See footnote 26, p. 110.

9. *Thailand*, p. 72. See also pp. 38, 58, and 103–4.

10. Christine Chapman, "Exam Hell in Japan" in *The Chronicle of Higher Education*, Volume XVIII, Number 7, October 16, 1978, p. 9.

11. *Japan*, p. 90.

12. *Federal Republic of Germany*, p. 92.

CHAPTER 8

1. *Poland*, p. 22.

2. Ibid., p. 56.

3. *Sweden*, Rune Premfors, pp. 132, 134.

4. *United States*, Lyman Glenny, p. 104. Glenny's reference is to a graph entitled "Ladd-Lipset Survey," in *The Chronicle for Higher Education*, Volume XV, Number 11, November 14, 1977, p. 2.

5. *United Kingdom*, Tony Becher, pp. 101–2.

6. *United States*, Alan Pifer, pp. 9–10.

7. *Federal Republic of Germany*, p. 5.

8. *Sweden*, Rune Premfors, p. 15. See also pp. 9, 27–28.

9. *Japan*, p. 97. The Report of the Central Council for Education to the Minister of Education, 1972, is carried as appendix I, pp. 95–130.

10. *United Kingdom*, Tony Becher, p. 102. See the section "Pursuit of Knowledge," pp. 100–4.

CHAPTER 9

1. *Poland*, p. 70.

2. *United States*, Lyman Glenny, pp. 97–98.

3. For an interesting analysis of historical development of power levels, see Burton R. Clark's chapter "Academic Power: Concepts, Modes, & Perspectives," in *Academic Power. Patterns of Authority in Seven National Systems of Higher Education* by John H. Van de Graaff, Burton R. Clark, Dorothea Furth, et al. (New York: Praeger Publishers, 1978), pp. 164–89. Also see Clark's "Coordination: Patterns and Processes," in *12 Systems of Higher Education: 6 Decisive Issues*, (New York: International Council for Educational Development, 1978), pp. 57–95.

4. *Sweden*, Bertil Östergren, pp. 169–70.

5. *United Kingdom*, Tony Becher, p. 112. See also Brian MacArthur "Flexibility and Innovation" in *12 Systems of Higher Education*, op. cit., pp. 117–18.

6. *Poland*, pp. 69–70.

7. *United Kingdom*, Tony Becher, pp. 118–19.

8. *United States*, Lyman Glenny, p. 98.

9. Ibid., pp. 100–1.

10. *France*, p. 31. See the whole passage, pp. 30–32.

11. Ibid., p. 33.

12. *United States*, Lyman Glenny, p. 99.

13. *Iran*, pp. 36–37.

14. *Australia*, p. 35.

15. *Sweden*, Rune Premfors, pp. 46–47.

16. *Federal Republic of Germany*, pp. 147–48. See the section on manpower, pp. 141–51.

17. *United Kingdom*, Tony Becher, p. 110.

18. *Canada*, Edward Sheffield, p. 200.

19. *Japan*, p. 49. See also Appendix II, p. 131.

20. *Thailand*, pp. 95–97.

21. *United States*, Lyman Glenny, p. 99.

22. *Federal Republic of Germanay*, pp. 129–32.

23. Brian MacArthur, "Flexibility and Innovation," in *12 Systems of Higher Education*, op. cit., p. 113. Brian MacArthur's statement is based on Clark Kerr's speech "Higher Education: Paradise Lost?" given at Uppsala University, September 28, 1977.

24. *Sweden*, Bertel Östergren, p. 169. See also Premfor's discussion of university branches, p. 9, and the changing age of students, p. 20.

25. *Canada*, Duncan D. Campbell, p. 151. See the section on Saskatchewan, pp. 146–53.

26. *Canada*, James H. Whitelaw, pp. 65–99. References to CEGEPs are throughout the section.

27. *United States*, Lyman Glenny, p. 101.

28. *Federal Republic of Germany*, pp. 124–25.

29. *Australia*, p. 83.

30. *Canada*, James H. Whitelaw, pp. 95–96.

31. *United Kingdom*, Tony Becher, p. 122.

32. *Federal Republic of Germany*, p. 129.

33. *France*, Appendix B, Title II, Article 6, p. 123.

34. *Sweden*, Bertil Östergren, p. 160. For the preceding statement on Swedish institutions, see p. 192.

35. *Federal Republic of Germany*, pp. 117–18.

36. Ibid., pp. 119–20. See full section on structural reform, pp. 117–25.

37. *Mexico*, pp. 62–63.

38. *Australia*, p. 85.

39. Ibid., p. 84.

40. Paul Woodring, *Investment in Innovation* (Boston: Little Brown, 1970), p. 142.

41. *Canada*, p. 60. For other facts in this paragraph on the use of television, see pp. 96, and 127–28.

42. *United Kingdom*, Tony Becher, pp. 116–17.

43. Nell Eurich and Barry Schwenkmeyer, *Great Britain's Open University: First Chance, Second Chance, or Last Chance?* (New York: Academy for Educational Development, 1971), pp. 3–5.

44. Brian MacArthur, "Flexibility and Innovation" in *12 Systems of Higher Education*, op. cit., pp. 103–4.

45. *Thailand, pp. 94, 113.*

46. *Iran*, pp. 30, 37.

47. *Federal Republic of Germany*, p. 128. See also footnote 20, p. 138.

48. Eurich and Schwenkmeyer, op. cit., p. 26.

Appendix A: Guidelines
for Country Studies

These guidelines represent the general content of the country studies. They are something less than rigid detailed requirements but considerably more than only general suggestions. We would like these guidelines to be observed with care but interpreted in a way that will provide the country director with flexibility to assure a good presentation of his country's system of higher education.

I. *The Design and Functions of the System of Higher Education*

This Section should be *descriptive* of the structure rather than an explanation as to *how* the system functions.

    A. *The Design*

        (a) *The Individual Institutions in the System*:

            What types? Universities, colleges, technical schools, special institutes, etc.?

            How many of each type?

            Total enrollments and budgets by types of institutions?

            Geographical dispersion? Urban and rural? Residential and commuting?

        (b) *Are There Private Institutions?*

            Percentage of total in numbers and enrollments. Are they secular or religious; included in the system or not? Describe.

        (c) *Institutional Governance*

            The roles of faculty, students, administration and governing/ advisory boards on the institutional level.

        (d) *Relationships of Institutions*

            To intermediate bodies and to central or state (provincial) governments.

B. *The Functions*

How are the purposes, the functions, of the system of higher education stated? You may wish to quote from relative documents or legislative statements where available on such purposes as:

(a) *Manpower*

The recruitment, sorting, training and certification of the trained manpower needed by society. The emphasis is on central planning.

(b) *Individual Development*

While manpower suggests a social need, individual development represents individual desires and expectations. The emphasis is on market demand.

(c) *Advancement and Diffusion of Knowledge*

The emphasis is on the content of education, the body of knowledge: research, scholarship and its uses.

(d) *Public Service*

The contribution of higher education to the solution of high priority public problems: science and defense, agriculture and starvation, medicine and public health.

II. *The Management of the System of Higher Education*

With respect to the structure outlined in I above, explain here the way in which the system is supposed to operate and how it really operates. Give attention to the following matters:

A. *Planning*

Where is the locus for system-wide planning:

(a) Legislative body, governmental agency or ministry, intermediate body, institutional administration or academic department?

(b) How does the informational or investigatory process operate as a basis for planning.

B. *Administration*

What is the process for the decision making? What levels are involved? Are the different constituencies represented with respect to the following:

(a) Preparation of budgets and the allocation of funds.

(b) Admission of students.

(c) Selection of faculty.

(d) Development and change in the curriculum.

(e) Establishment of new institutions.

C. *Coordination*

1. For systems that are moving from institutional autonomy to system-wide planning and management, describe the various ways that structures and procedures have evolved (and are evolving) to achieve this purpose:

(a) The risk of intermediary bodies. What form have these taken? How are they governed, staffed, and positioned between government and individual institutions?

    (b) How does the intermediary body handle relations with government?

    (c) How does it relate to the individual institutions it is supposed to coordinate? What are the points of friction?

    (d) The special problems of federal, decentralized systems.

2. For systems that are searching for ways to reduce central authority, what are the problems involved and how are they being handled?

    (a) Regionalism or geographical decentralization? Can structural decentralization be accomplished without financial decentralization? Do faculty and students favor or resist? Why?

    (b) Institutional autonomy—Is this considered desirable generally or only in certain areas? How can it be effected?

    (c) The special problems of unitary, centralized systems.

III. *Effectiveness of the System of Higher Education*

  A. In determining the effectiveness of the system in carrying out the social purposes, the following questions should be examined:

    (a) Does the system discover and produce the human talent required to serve the manpower needs of the country? If yes, what features of the system are most helpful? If not, where are the difficulties? What improvements can be made?

    (b) Is the system just? Is there equal opportunity for equal talent? Are there educational institutions and programs that match the different needs and preparations of student applicants?

    (c) Is there a constructive relationship between advanced education and research? How, at what levels, and by what processes and using what criteria are research funds allocated to universities? Or is research, particularly basic research, carried on outside the universities? With what consequences?

    (d) Does the system make an effective contribution to social problems of high priority? Are these priorities part of the plans and planning?

  B. Is the system flexible and innovative? Higher education is known for its difficulty in effecting change, whether improvement of the present system and curricula or the inauguration of new programs designed to provide for emerging societal needs.

    (a) Does the system provide a mechanism or plan to facilitate innovation as well as minor change and adaptation? Where does the initiative lie for curricular innovation? Have faculty and students a role? For structural change in the system are government bodies determining?

(b) Give evidence or examples of innovative change recently and explain how it was accomplished both formally and informally. Or show how it failed and why.

(c) Do forces external to the system play a significant role in prompting or defeating a change?

C. Is the system efficient? Recognizing the difficulties in judging efficiency in large, widespread organizational structures with many levels of operation and human talents, evaluate generally the effectiveness of management and operations as reflected in these following areas. Indicate those areas where the process seems to work more smoothly and the work is accomplished without undue delay and those areas where greater difficulties exist. Explain.

(a) Planning functions.

(b) Administrative functions and decisions making in the areas enumerated in section IIB above.

(c) Coordinating functions in either decentralized or centralized systems.

D. *Other Comments*

Appendix B.: Lists of
Country Studies

COUNTRY	SPONSOR	DIRECTOR OF STUDY
Australia	University of Sydney	Bruce Williams and Assessors
Canada	Higher Education Group, University of Toronto	Edward Sheffield and Panel
Federal Republic of Germany	Zentrum I Bildungsforschung, University of Konstanz	Hansgert Peisert and Gerhild Framhein
France	Secretary of State for Higher Education	Alain Bienaymé and Panel
Iran	Ministry of Science and Education	A. H. Samii and Panel
Japan	National Institute for Educational Research	Isai Amagi K. Narita, and Staff
Mexico	Asociación de Universidades e Institutos de Enseñanza Superior	Alfonso Rangel Guerra
Poland	Institute for Higher Education Research	Jan Szczepański
Sweden	The Office of the Chancellor of the Swedish Universities	Bertil Östergren
Thailand	National Education Commission	Sippanondha Ketudat and Panel
United Kingdom	Committee of Vice-Chancellors	Tony Becher and Panel
United States	International Council for Educational Development	James A. Perkins and Panel

About the Author

For the past five years NELL EURICH has been senior consultant to the International Council for Educational Development. She is also a trustee of several higher education institutions. Previous experience includes teaching and administrative posts at both public and private institutions. She was Dean of Faculty at Vassar College and Provost and Academic Vice President at Manhattanville College. Dr. Eurich has served on numerous national commissions such as the Carnegie Council on Policy Studies in Higher Education, and she has held governmental appointments from the U.S. Department of State, the Department of Health, Education, and Welfare, and the National Endowment for the Humanities. She has participated internationlly in conferences on higher education issues in Poland, Mexico, Australia, Japan, Iran, and England. Dr. Eurich holds advanced degrees from Stanford University and Columbia University.